THE VITAL GUIDE TO

MODERN WARSHIPS

EDITOR: LEO MARRIOTT

Airlife
England

Copyright © 2001 Airlife Publishing Ltd

First published in the UK in 2001
by Airlife Publishing Ltd

British Library Cataloguing-in-Publication Data
A catalogue record for this book
is available from the British Library

ISBN 1 84037 177 3

Typeset by Echelon, Wimborne
Printed in Hong Kong

Airlife Publishing Ltd
101 Longden Road, Shrewsbury,
SY3 9EB, England
E-mail: airlife@airlifebooks.com
Website: www.airlifebooks.com

CONTENTS

Notes on Data Tables

The following notes apply to the data provided in the description of each warship type listed in the following pages.

Type:
The standard NATO designations are used to describe the function of the ship (see Glossary).

Nationality:
Normally the country which is the major user of the relevant warship class, although the country of construction may also be indicated.

Class:
The name which refers to the group of ships of the same design. Most are normally named after the lead ship, although a generic designation may be applied (e.g Type 42).

Displacement:
Unless otherwise indicated, the figure given is the standard displacement.

Length, Beam and Draught:
Measurements given in feet and metres to one point of decimals. Unless otherwise specified, length refers to overall length, beam to the widest part of the hull and draught to keel depth.

Machinery:
Propulsion type. Power ratings relate to maximum available continuous power which may be less than the peak figure sometimes quoted.

Speed:
Maximum unless otherwise specified.

Armament:
Described under Missiles and Guns, together with a section describing any anti-submarine or underwater weapons systems such as torpedoes, mortars and decoys.

Sensors:
Describes radar and sonar systems fitted.

Aircraft:
Figure quoted is normally the maximum number which can be embarked.

INTRODUCTION

The modern warship is a complex vessel. In the last thirty years the pace of change and development has greatly increased as new technologies, including electronics, missiles, propulsion and hydrodynamics, have been applied to make each ship more effective than its predecessor. As in any form of warfare, there is a constant struggle to upset the balance between attack and defence, and the situation is made more complex by the fact that warships must basically fight in three separate environments: on the surface of the sea, under the surface and in the air above. Here, the reader is presented with a representative sample of modern warships although, in a book this size, it would be impossible to describe every type of warship in use. There are literally hundreds of warship and submarine classes in service today, so some type of selection has been necessary in order to reduce these to manageable proportions. In general, therefore, the most modern and up-to-date vessels are described, although it has been necessary to include some older ships where these have a particular operational significance. For example, many of the current US Navy aircraft carriers are over thirty years old but are still among the most powerful warships in existence. Some other major warship classes are included where they are operationally significant, despite being relatively long in the tooth.

In order to give a balanced picture, it is not only the major vessels which are described but also representative samples of smaller warships, including fast and well-armed corvettes or fast attack craft, as well as often overlooked, but vital, mine warfare vessels. A major function of modern navies is power projection, the ability to transfer and support significant land, sea and air forces to any part of the world within reach of the sea. In modern littoral warfare, this can include objectives up to 150 miles (240km) inland and involves the deployment of purpose-built amphibious warfare vessels, examples of which are also described. Finally, the ocean is a large place and the distances to be covered are great, often taking warships thousands of miles away from their home bases. In such situations the presence of a well-equipped logistics system is vital and this can also act as a force multiplier as well as merely providing supplies. A representative selection of logistic support vessels is therefore also included.

For convenience and ease of reference, the ships described in the main body of this book are grouped according to the following broad classifications: Aircraft Carriers, Submarines, Major Warships, Destroyers and Frigates, Small Warships, Amphibious Warfare and Logistic Support. In each group, the ships are presented in descending order of size as indicated by their standard displacement.

AIRCRAFT CARRIERS

Major vessels equipped with continuous flightdecks whose purpose is the operation and support of naval fixed-wing aircraft and helicopters. Their main functions include air defence of naval forces by establishing local air superiority, offensive operations against enemy naval forces, support of amphibious landings, support of ground operations ashore, anti-submarine warfare and reconnaissance. The most significant ships in this group are the large nuclear-powered carriers of the US Navy, Russian attempts to compete having collapsed after the end of the Cold War in the early 1990s. The only other country which currently has a substantial conventional aircraft carrier is France, although the UK plans two 40,000-ton carriers for service around 2013. The development of a viable vertical take-off aircraft in the form of the Sea Harrier and the later AV-8A/B has enabled a number of other navies to aspire to carrier aviation. These include the UK with its three Invincible class ships, Spain, Italy and Thailand. India also has an ex-British carrier and is planning to acquire one of the larger Russian carriers, which is now available, although this will operate the potent supersonic MiG-29K.

CVN, Nimitz

THERE ARE CURRENTLY EIGHT of these massive nuclear-powered aircraft carriers in service with the US Navy. A ninth, USS *Ronald Reagan* (CVN-76), is under construction while CVN-77 was authorised in 1999 but will not commission until 2008. Originally the first three were known as the Nimitz class after the lead ship was completed in 1975, the others being the *Dwight D. Eisenhower* (1977) and *Carl Vinson* (1982). Subsequent vessels formed the Theodore Roosevelt class. However, apart from an increased full load displacement and many detail differences, they are now regarded as a single class for operational purposes. The *Theodore Roosevelt* commissioned in 1986, followed by the *Abraham Lincoln* (1989), *George Washington* (1992), *John C. Stennis* (1995) and *Harry S. Truman* (1998).

These carriers are the largest warships ever built and their nuclear reactors have an expected life of up to 15 years, representing around one million miles between refuelling. The 4.5-acre (18,200m²) flightdeck is home to up to 80 aircraft of the assigned carrier air wing (CVW) which typically includes 50 fighters and strike aircraft (F-14 Tomcat and F-18 Hornet) as well as electronic warfare, AEW and ASW aircraft and helicopters. These are organised into 10 separate squadrons and most of the aircraft are usually ranged on deck as the hangars, despite their size, can accommodate no more than half this total. Three deck-edge lifts on the starboard side and one on the port side are provided for the transfer of aircraft between flightdeck and hangars. There are four Type C Mk.13 Mod 1 steam catapults which can accelerate the heaviest aircraft to a speed in excess of 170mph (270kph) within 3 seconds through a stroke of 310ft (95m). For landing, there are four arrester wires which can bring an aircraft to rest from a landing speed of 160mph (260kph) within a distance 300ft (91m).

The last ship to be built, CVN-77, will be laid down in 2003 and completion is planned for 2008. Originally this was to have been to a new CVX design, but instead CVN-77 will be based upon the basic Nimitz design and will carry new equipment and systems, possibly including electromagnetic catapults instead of the current steam catapults. The design of the island superstructure will also be altered, and may be broken up into several smaller structures.

USS Abraham Lincoln, *Nimitz* class CVN.
(Public Affairs Office, USS Abraham Lincoln)

USS Nimitz, CVN-68.
(Public Affairs Office, USS Nimitz)

SPECIFICATION

Type: CVN
Class: Nimitz
Displacement: 102,000 tons full load
Length: 1,092ft (317m)
Beam: wl 134ft (40.8m), flightdeck 252ft (76.8m)
Draught: 39ft (11.9m)
Machinery: nuclear; 2 Westinghouse/GE A1G PWR reactors; 4 turbines, 260,000hp; 4 emergency diesels, 10,720hp; 4 shafts
Speed & Range: 30kt +; 15 years between reactor refuelling
Complement: 5,930 (including air group and staff)
Missiles: 3 Mk.29 octuple launchers, Sea Sparrow short-range SAM; RAM short-range SAM being fitted
Guns: 4 Vulcan/Phalanx 6-barrelled 20mm CIWS
ASW & USW: SSTDS torpedo defence system; SLQ-36 Nixie torpedo decoy
Sensors: radar: SPS-48E long-range 3D air search; SPS-49 air search; Mk.23 target acquisition; SPS-67 surface search; SPN43B, SPN46 aircraft control; SPS-64 and Furuno 900 navigation; Mk.95 fire control
Aircraft: 70 fixed-wing aircraft, 10 helicopters (typical air wing)
(Note: data applies to *Abraham Lincoln* and later ships)

USS Abraham Lincoln, *Nimitz* class CVN.
(Public Affairs Office, USS Abraham Lincoln)

CVN, Enterprise

THE USS *ENTERPRISE*, CVN-65, was the US Navy's first nuclear-powered aircraft carrier. She was laid down in February 1958, was launched on 24 September 1960 and commissioned on 25 November 1961, an amazingly short period in which to build such a complex and advanced warship. In fact she was the world's second nuclear-powered surface warship, the first being the cruiser *Long Beach*. Since entering service the *Enterprise* has undergone several refits and modernisation programmes, and is today very similar in terms of combat capability to the later Nimitz class. She is likely to remain in service for the foreseeable future as long as the US Navy retains its stated requirement for a 12-carrier force. Allowing for two on extended refit at any given time, and others undergoing trials and operational training, this allows for around five or six continuously available for operational deployments.

The *Enterprise*, whose name commemorates a very famous US Navy carrier in World War II which took part in virtually all of the major actions in the Pacific and survived unscathed until retirement in 1947, carries a standard carrier air wing (CVW) of around 76 to 80 aircraft. She cost around $450 million to build, an extremely high figure for the time and almost twice the price of the conventionally powered Kittyhawk class. Plans for five sister ships were as a result abandoned, and a gap of 10 years elapsed between the laying down of the *Enterprise* in 1958 and the first of the Nimitz class. The *Enterprise* was constructed by Newport News Shipbuilding, the only yard capable of building such large warships, and all the Nimitz class ships were also built here. Fittingly, the planned replacement for the *Enterprise* will be the first of a new class of carriers, CVNX-1. This will retain the basic Nimitz class layout but will have a new-design nuclear plant and advanced features such as electromagnetic aircraft launching systems (EMALS). Another design target will be a significant reduction in the ship's complement, possibly by as much as 50%.

USS Enterprise *(CVN-65), the first nuclear-powered aircraft carrier.*
(US Navy)

SPECIFICATION

Type: CVN
Class: Enterprise
Displacement: 75,700 tons standard, 93,970 tons full load
Length: 1,123ft (342.3m)
Beam: wl 133ft (40.5m), flightdeck 252ft (76.8m)
Draught: 39ft (11.9m)
Machinery: nuclear; 2 Westinghouse/GE A2W PWR reactors; 4 turbines, 280,000hp; 4 emergency diesels, 10,720hp; 4 shafts
Speed & Range: 33kt
Complement: 5,765 (including air group and staff)
Missiles: 3 Mk.29 octuple launchers, Sea Sparrow short-range SAM
Guns: 3 Vulcan/Phalanx 6-barrelled 20mm CIWS
ASW & USW: SSTDS torpedo defence system; SLQ-36 Nixie torpedo decoy
Sensors: radar: SPS-48E long-range 3D air search; SPS-49 air search; Mk.23 target acquisition; SPS-67 surface search; SPN43A, SPN46 aircraft control; SPS-64 and Furuno 900 navigation; Mk.95 fire control
Aircraft: typical air wing includes 72 fixed-wing aircraft, 6 helicopters

CV, Kittyhawk/Kennedy

IN THE AFTERMATH OF WORLD WAR II, in the late 1950s, the US Navy introduced the Forrestal class of four large 'super carriers', the first to be designed from the start to operate the new generations of naval jets then entering service. These have now all been decommissioned but they were followed by three larger ships of the Kittyhawk class which were completed between 1961 and 1965. Construction of the fourth ship, USS *John F. Kennedy*, was delayed by a debate over whether it was to be nuclear-powered, although eventually it was completed in 1968 with conventional steam turbine machinery.

Kittyhawk and *Constellation* saw considerable service in the Vietnam War, each spending several periods of duty in that theatre up to 1972, when American forces withdrew. The USS *America*, one of the three Kittyhawk class ships, was withdrawn from service in 1996, and the *John F. Kennedy* is held in reserve status. *Kittyhawk* is based in Japan with her carrier air wing, CVW-5, deployed ashore at Atsugi air base. *Constellation* and *Kittyhawk* underwent modernisation in service life extension programmes (SLEP), completed in 1992 and 1991 respectively. This effectively brought the ships up to the same standard as the Nimitz class in terms of communications and electronic systems, as well as defensive armament and aircraft operating equipment.

It is sobering to realise that these ships, originally commissioned in 1961, are now 40 years old but still capable of operating the latest aircraft. These include the F-14 Tomcat and the F/A-18 Hornet fixed-wing fighters and attack aircraft, as well as EA-6B Prowlers for electronic warfare, E-2C Hawkeye AEW aircraft, S-3B Viking ASW aircraft, and SH/HH-60 Seahawk helicopters. Despite being slightly smaller than the later Nimitz class, the *Kittyhawk* and her sisters carry identical air groups, although storage for aviation fuel and ordnance is somewhat less.

USS *Constellation* is due to decommission in 2003 when it will be replaced by USS *Ronald Reagan* (CVN-76). The more advanced CVN-77 will replace the USS *Kittyhawk* in 2008, and the USS *John F. Kennedy* will be succeeded by CVNX-2 in 2018.

USS* Kittyhawk *(CV-63) photographed in the Persian Gulf in company with the British RFA Brambleleaf. (US Navy)

USS* Kittyhawk *entering Pearl Harbor. F-14 Tomcats, F-18 Hornets and E-6 Prowlers are ranged on the flightdeck. (US Navy)

USS* John F. Kennedy *(CV-67). (US Navy)

SPECIFICATION

Type: CV
Class: Kittyhawk/Kennedy
Displacement: 81,430 tons full load
Length: 1,052ft (320.6m)
Beam: wl 130ft (39.6m), flightdeck 252ft (76.8m)
Draught: 37.4ft (11.4m)
Machinery: 8 boilers, 4 Westinghouse turbines, 280,000hp; 4 shafts
Speed & Range: 32kt; 12,000 miles (19,300km) at 20kt
Complement: 5,520 (including air wing and staff)
Missiles: 3 Mk.29 octuple launchers, Sea Sparrow short-range SAM
Guns: 3 or 4 Vulcan/Phalanx 6-barrelled 20mm CIWS
ASW & USW: SSTDS torpedo defence system; SLQ-36 Nixie torpedo decoy
Sensors: radar: SPS-48E long-range 3D air search; SPS-49 air search; Mk.23 target acquisition; SPS-67 surface search; SPN43A, SPN46 aircraft control; SPS-64 and Furuno 900 navigation; Mk.95 fire control
Aircraft: typical air wing includes 72 fixed-wing aircraft, 6–8 helicopters

CV, Admiral Kuznetzov

ORIGINALLY LAID DOWN IN 1983, this is Russia's only surviving aircraft carrier. A sister ship, the *Varying*, was never completed and three smaller Kiev class aircraft-carrying cruisers are all non-operational. One of these, the *Admiral Gorshkov*, is being sold to India after a modernisation refit which will include the removal of some long-range missile systems to allow the flightdeck to be extended to the bow.

The current *Admiral Kuznetzov* (originally named *Tblisi*) normally carries an air group comprising 18 to 24 Sukhoi Su-33 Flanker D fighters of the 279th Shipboard Fighter Aviation Regiment, four Sukhoi Su-25UTG Frogfoot ground attack and training aircraft, and up to 15 Kamov Ka-27 Helix ASW helicopters and two Ka-31 RLD AEW helicopters. The flightdeck layout is closely based on that of contemporary American carriers but differs in that a ski-jump ramp is incorporated at the bow, a feature normally associated with STOVL aircraft such as the Sea Harrier. The *Kuznetzov* was originally designed with the Yak-38M (similar to the Sea Harrier) in mind, and this may account for the ramp, although it appears to work just as well with the conventional take-off of the Su-33, a much larger and heavier aircraft.

In contrast to the American carriers, which rely exclusively on the aircraft for offensive strike, the *Kuznetzov* carries a substantial battery of SS-N-19 Shipwreck anti-ship missiles with a maximum range of almost 250 miles (400km). More significantly, these can carry 500-kiloton nuclear warheads. The missiles are carried in a silo flush mounted below the forward flightdeck. For self-defence the ship carries substantial batteries of short-range SSMs including the SA-N-9 Gauntlet with a range of six to seven miles (11km) and the SA-N-11 Grisson, with a range of four to five miles (8km). The latter are carried on a combined mounting with AK360 30mm CIWS gun systems. Altogether, the *Kuznetzov* would prove a prickly target to attack, and in wartime the aircraft complement would be boosted to around 60 aircraft and helicopters. However, lack of funding presently severely restricts the operation of this ship, which has spent relatively little time at sea since it was first commissioned in 1991.

Admiral Kuznetzov.
(RAF Kinloss/MoD)

***Hormone ASW helicopters aboard the* Admiral Kuznetzov.**
(via Naval Technology)

SPECIFICATION

Type: CV
Class: Admiral Kuznetzov
Displacement: 45,000 tons (standard), 58,500 tons (full load)
Length: oa and flightdeck 999ft (304.5m), wl 918.6ft (280m)
Beam: oa 229.7ft (70m), wl 121.4ft (37m)
Draught: 34ft (10.36m)
Machinery: 4 steam turbines (8 boilers), each 50,000hp; 4 shafts
Speed & Range: 30kt; 3,850 miles (6,195km) at 29kt, 8,500 miles (13,675km) at 18kt
Complement: 1,960 + air group
Missiles: 12 single launchers, SS-N-19 Shipwreck long-range SSM; 4 sextuple launchers, Altair SA-N-9 Gauntlet short-range SAM ten-tube launchers, Altair SA-N-11 Grisson short-range SAM
Guns: 8 twin Gatling type 30mm guns (co-mounted with SA-N-11 missile launchers) 6 six-barrelled AK630 30mm CIWS
ASW & USW: 2 RBU 12000 A/S mortars; UDAV-1M torpedo countermeasures
Sensors: radars: Sky Watch Planar Array air search; Top Plate B air/surface search; Strut Pair surface search; Palm Frond navigation; Cross Sword and Hot Flash fire control; Fly Trap aircraft control; sonar: Bull Horn and Horse Jaw, hull-mounted active search and attack
Aircraft: 22 fixed-wing, 17 helicopters

FRANCE
CVN, Charles de Gaulle

IN 1980 THE FRENCH DEFENCE COUNCIL approved a plan to build two nuclear-powered aircraft carriers to replace the *Clemenceau* and *Foch*, which had entered service in the early 1960s. Eventually only one ship, to be named *Charles de Gaulle*, was ordered in 1986, although the formal keel laying was not until April 1989. Thereafter work progressed slowly, often delayed by financial problems, and the ship was not launched until 7 May 1994 and did not commission following initial sea trials until March 2000. Plans for a second ship are in abeyance, and any order is unlikely to be placed until around 2005 at the earliest. The cost of building the *Charles de Gaulle* has had a major effect on French naval planning and plans to retain the *Foch* as a reserve carrier have been abandoned – *Foch* has now been sold to the Brazilian Navy and will re-enter service in 2002 after a refit. The *Clemenceau* has already been discarded and the result will be that the French Navy will now have only one operational carrier for the foreseeable future, although, admittedly, it is an extremely powerful one.

The air group will eventually comprise some 40 aircraft which will initially be made up of mainly nuclear-capable Super Etendard strike aircraft, but these will be joined by a squadron of the multi-role Rafale M in 2001. Some 60 Rafales are on order but delivery of these will not be completed until the next decade, by which time they will have completely supplanted the Super Etendards. In addition the French Navy has purchased four E-2C Hawkeye AEW aircraft although the flightdeck has proved to be a few metres too short for normal operations by this type of aircraft and will be lengthened by four metres at an early opportunity. Initially, Panther and Super Frelon helicopters will be embarked, but these will both eventually be replaced by the multi-role NH90 when deliveries begin in 2003.

Following initial sea trials in 1999, the ship docked for a six-month refit at the end of the year to rectify problems with rudder vibration at high speed and other deficiencies highlighted by the trials, and

Charles de Gaulle, *France's nuclear-powered aircraft carrier, undergoing sea trials.* (Marine Nationale, France)

to upgrade the command and control facilities. On completion of this work she was formally commissioned in October 2000 and was ready to begin working up the air group to full operational standard. Despite the cost overruns and publicised teething troubles, the completion of this ship is a major achievement for the French shipbuilding industry and places the *Marine Nationale* in the forefront of current naval aviation practice, although the lack of a sister ship will restrict operational availability.

SPECIFICATION

Type: CVN
Class: Charles de Gaulle
Displacement: 36,600 tons standard, 40,550 tons full load
Length: oa and flightdeck 857.7ft (261.5m), wl 780.8ft (238m)
Beam: oa 211.3ft (64.4m), wl 103.3ft (31.5m)
Draught: 27.8ft (8.5m)
Machinery: nuclear; 2 PWR Type K15 reactors, 300MW; 2 GEC Alsthom steam turbines, 76,200hp; 2 shafts
Speed & Range: 27kt; 5 years steaming at 20kt
Complement: 1,150 + 600 air group and staff
Missiles: 4 EUROSAM octuple VLS launchers, Aster 15 anti-missile and SAM; 2 Sadral PDMS sextuple launchers, Mistral short-range SAM
Guns: 8 Giat 20F2 20mm guns
ASW & USW: SLAT torpedo decoys
Sensors: radar: Thompson CSF DRBJ 11B medium-/long-range air search, DBRV 26D Jupiter medium-range air search, DRBV 15D Sea Tiger medium-range air search, Racal 1229 (DRBN 34A) navigation, Thompson CSF Arabel fire control; sonar: SLAT torpedo warning
Aircraft: 35–40 fixed-wing plus helicopters

A Hawkeye E-2C AEW aircraft landing aboard the Charles de Gaulle. (Marine Nationale, France)

CV, Viraat

A bow view of INS Viraat, *previously* HMS Hermes *of the Royal Navy. (Mike Lennon)*

ORIGINALLY LAID DOWN IN 1944, this ship was completed for the Royal Navy as HMS *Hermes* in 1959. After a long and varied career, including a key role in the 1982 Falklands War, she was decommissioned and sold to India in 1986. Following a refit and modest modernisation programme, she recommissioned as INS *Viraat* on 20 May 1987.

Externally, the ship differs little in appearance from her British service and, in particular, retains the distinctive ski-jump ramp fitted at the bows to facilitate the launch of fully loaded Sea Harriers. The Indian Navy currently operates approximately 23 Sea Harrier FRS.51 single-seaters and a number of two-seat trainers. The FRS.51 is the equivalent of the Royal Navy's FRS.1 which has now been superseded by the more advanced F/A.2 variant. Plans to similarly upgrade the Indian aircraft are awaiting the necessary funding, although the existing aircraft are armed with the potent Sea Eagle anti-ship missile as well as air-to-air missiles, conventional bombs and 30mm cannon. In the meantime two squadrons, each of six Sea Harriers, normally serve aboard the *Viraat*, together with various ASW helicopters including Sea King Mk.42s or Kamov Ka-28 Helixs. India is also taking delivery of four Kamov Ka-31 Helix AEW helicopters which will provide a substantial boost to the effectiveness of the Sea Harriers.

A second Indian carrier was the *Vikrant*, an ex-British Majestic class light fleet carrier originally laid down in 1943 but only completed in 1961. This ship was decommissioned in 1996, since when India has actively sought a second carrier. Various options were investigated, including the building of a conventionally powered version of the French *Charles de Gaulle*. However, India has completed negotiations to purchase the Russian *Admiral Gorshkov* in a deal which also involves the acquisition of Su-30K or MiG-29K high-performance fighters. As this plan is implemented, it may mean the end of a project to build a 24,000-ton air defence ship in India.

SPECIFICATION

Type: CV
Class: Viraat
Displacement: 23,900 tons standard, 28,700 tons full load
Length: 744.3ft (226.9m)
Beam: wl 90ft (27.4m), flightdeck 160ft (48.8m)
Draught: 28.5ft (8.7m)
Machinery: 4 boilers, 2 Parsons steam turbines, 76,000hp; 2 shafts
Speed & Range: 28kt
Complement: 1,350
Missiles: nil
Guns: 2 Bofors 40mm/60; 2 AK230 30mm multi-barrelled guns
ASW & USW: nil
Sensors: radar: Type 966 long-range air search; DA05 air and surface search; Type 1006 navigation; sonar: Type 184M hull-mounted active search and attack
Aircraft: 12 (30 max.) fixed-wing, 7 helicopters

CVS, Invincible

THESE SHIPS WERE CONCEIVED in the late 1960s following the cancellation of the CVA-01 class of fleet carriers in 1966. The prime requirement was to provide a platform to carry and operate viable numbers of the large Sea King anti-submarine helicopter. For political reasons the ships were known as through-deck command cruisers (TDCC) and facilities for conventional fixed-wing aircraft were not included in the design. However, the development of the Sea Harrier VTOL jet fighter in the 1970s enabled the Royal Navy to restore some organic air defence to its fleet when HMS *Invincible* commissioned in 1980.

The value of the Sea Harrier (and the ground attack RAF Harrier GR3) was clearly demonstrated in operations to recover the Falklands following the Argentine invasion in 1982. Together with the elderly HMS *Hermes*, the *Invincible* played a crucial part in the war, its Sea Harriers providing air defence for the fleet and support for the troops ashore. The second ship of the class, HMS *Illustrious*, commissioned just too late to see service in the Falklands, but was rushed to the South Atlantic to relieve *Invincible* when she returned home after spending 166 days continuously at sea, a record for any British aircraft carrier. A third ship, *Ark Royal*, was completed and commissioned in 1985, since when there have normally been two of the class in commission with the third in reserve or undergoing refit.

The normal air group was established at eight Sea Harriers, nine ASW Sea Kings and two AEW Sea Kings. However, in 1998/99, HMS *Illustrious* was modified by removing the Sea Dart missile launcher and associated magazines from the bows in order to increase flightdeck area forward, as well as providing additional storage for aircraft ordnance. She can now support an additional six aircraft in the form of RAF Harrier GR strike aircraft in addition to eight or nine upgraded Sea Harrier F/A.2s. *Ark Royal* is being similarly refitted, work due to be completed in May 2001, with *Invincible* to follow.

HMS Illustrious, showing new flightdeck extension. (Royal Navy)

HMS Illustrious, Invincible class CVS. (Royal Navy)

The United Kingdom is currently planning to build two 40,000-ton aircraft carriers to enter service from 2013. These will eventually replace the three Invincible class aircraft carriers.

SPECIFICATION

Type: CVS
Class: Invincible
Displacement: 20,600 tons full load
Length: oa 685.8ft (209.1m), wl 632ft (192.6m), flightdeck 550ft (167.8m)
Beam: oa 118ft (36m), wl 90ft (27.5m)
Draught: 26ft (8m)
Machinery: COGAG; 4 Rolls-Royce Olympus TM3B gas turbines, 97,000hp; 2 shafts
Speed & Range: 28kt; 7,000 miles (11,260km) at 19kt
Complement: 685 + air group
Missiles: Sea Dart medium-range surface-to-air missile system, 1 twin launcher (removed in some vessels)
Guns: 3 20mm Vulcan/Phalanx CIWS or 3 30mm Goalkeeper CIWS
ASW & USW: nil
Sensors: radars: Type 1022 air search, Type 996 surface search, Type 1006/7 navigation, Type 909 fire control; sonar: hull-mounted Type 2016 active search and attack
Aircraft: 15 fixed-wing STOVL, 9 helicopters (max.)

CVS, Príncipe de Asturias

THIS SHIP WAS BUILT BY BAZÁN at Ferrol in north-west Spain and its design was based on a 1970s US project for a Sea Control Ship, the main difference being the addition of a 12° ski-jump ramp at the bow to allow operation of Harriers. She was laid down on 8 October 1979, launched on 22 May 1982 and finally commissioned on 30 May 1988.

The air group composition varies with a fixed-wing element comprising 6 to 12 AV-8B Harrier II/Plus STOVL jet fighters and up to 10 helicopters including SH-3 Sea Kings operating in the ASW and AEW roles, Agusta Bell AB 212s for electronic warfare and SH-60B Seahawks also for ASW. Up to 37 aircraft in total could be embarked in an emergency, but a more typical mix would be eight Harriers (known as the Matador in Spanish service) and 10 helicopters. The main axis of the flightdeck is angled, unusually, to starboard to allow parking and operation of the stern lift to the hangar during flying operations. Another lift is positioned on the starboard side, immediately forward of the island. The island superstructure was enlarged during a 1990 refit to incorporate additional briefing rooms and covered parking for the flightdeck vehicles. For self-defence the ship carries the Spanish-designed Meroka CIWS which has a 12-barrelled 20mm gun firing 3,600 rounds per minute to a range of 1.25 miles (2km). Two mountings are carried on the stern and one on either beam near the bow, giving a complete 360° coverage.

The ship is normally deployed as the centrepiece of a powerful battle group which also includes up to five missile-armed frigates, and it was hoped that a second ship might have been built but, to date, the necessary funding has not been forthcoming. The *Príncipe de Asturias* has been very successful in service and a smaller version has been built for Thailand.

Príncipe de Asturias *(R11), showing the upswept ski-jump ramp at the bow. (author)*

Príncipe de Asturias *(foreground) in company with* **Chakri Narubet** *of the Thai Navy. (Bazán)*

Príncipe de Asturias *with Harriers embarked. (Mönch Archives)*

SPECIFICATION

Type: CVS
Class: Príncipe de Asturias
Displacement: 17,188 tons full load
Length: oa 642.7ft (195.8m), pp 615.2ft (187.5m), flightdeck 575.1ft (175.3m)
Beam: hull 79.7ft (24.3m), flightdeck 95.1ft (29m)
Draught: 30.8ft (9.4m)
Machinery: 2 GE LM2500 gas turbines, 46,400hp; single shaft with controllable pitch propeller; 2 1,600 electric motors driving a single retractable propeller
Speed & Range: 25kt; 6,500 miles (10,460km) at 20kt
Complement: 555 + 208 staff and air group
Missiles: nil
Guns: 4 Bazan Meroka 12-barrelled 20mm CIWS; 2 37mm saluting guns
ASW & USW: SLQ-25 Nixie towed torpedo decoy; US Prairie/Masker underwater noise suppression system
Sensors: radar: Hughes SPS-52C/D 3D long-range air search, ISC Cardion SPS-55 surface search, ITT SPN-35A aircraft control, Selenia RAN 12L target designator, RTN 11L missile warning, Sperry/Lockheed VPS2 fire control
Aircraft: 6–12 fixed-wing, up to 16 helicopters

CVS, Garibaldi

THIS IS A CAPABLE SHIP which packs a lot into a relatively small hull. Laid down at the Italcantieri yard at Monfalcone on 26 March 1981, the *Giuseppe Garibaldi* was launched on 4 June 1983 and commissioned on 30 September 1985. Initially the ship was employed as a helicopter carrier only with SH-3D Sea Kings and Agusta Bell AB 212 helicopters in the ASW role. It could also act as a helicopter assault ship and embarked army-operated AB 205 and A 129 attack helicopters as well as troop-carrying CH-47s. Deployment of fixed-wing aircraft was delayed until a dispute between the air force and navy as to who would operate such aircraft was finally resolved in favour of the navy in 1989. This allowed the purchase of 16 Boeing (McDonnell Douglas) AV-8B Harrier IIs to go ahead. In theory all of these can be embarked at once, but a more typical air group would comprise a mix of 18 Harriers and helicopters. The SH-3D Sea Kings will shortly be replaced by the larger Anglo-Italian EH101 Merlin helicopter in both AEW and ASW variants. For the future, Italy may order the JSF (Joint Strike Fighter) currently under development by the US and Britain as a replacement for the Harriers.

The 570ft (173m) flightdeck has a slight ski-jump ramp, angled at 6.5°, on the bows but the island superstructure is obtrusive and rather wide in proportion to overall beam. Lifts immediately fore and

Giuseppe Garibaldi, *Italy's first operational aircraft carrier.* (Marina Militare, Italy)

aft of the island serve the hangar deck, which can accommodate 10 Harriers or 12 Sea Kings.

The *Giuseppe Garibaldi* is Italy's first operational aircraft carrier, although in World War II a passenger liner was converted into the 23,350-ton carrier *Aquila* which never saw service and was eventually damaged in various attacks and scuttled. Currently a new 20,000-ton carrier will be laid down in 2002 for completion in 2006/7. Named *Luigi Einaudi*, it will carry up to 20 aircraft and helicopters.

SPECIFICATION

Type: CVS
Class: Garibaldi
Displacement: 10,100 tons standard, 13,850 tons full load
Length: oa 591.2ft (180m), flightdeck 570.2ft (173.8m)
Beam: oa 110.2ft (33.4m), flightdeck 99.7ft (30.4m)
Draught: 22ft (6.7m)
Machinery: COGAG; 4 Fiat/GE LM2500 gas turbines, 81,000hp; 2 shafts
Speed & Range: 30kt; 7,000 miles (11,260km) at 20kt
Complement: 550 + 230 air group
Missiles: 4 fixed launchers for OTO Melera Teseo Mk.2 long-range SSM octuple Albatros launchers, Aspide short-range SAM
Guns: 3 twin Breda 40mm/70 guns
ASW & USW: 2 324mm (12.75in) B-515 triple launchers, Mk.46 ASW torpedoes; SLQ-25 Nixie decoys
Sensors: radar: Hughes SPS-52C 3D long-range air search, Selenia SPS-768 medium-range air search, SPN-728 air search, Selenia SPS-774 air and surface search, SPS-702 target indication, SPN-749 navigation, SPG-75/RTN 30X missile control, SPG-74 fire control, SPN-728 aircraft control; sonars: Raytheon DE1160LF bow-mounted medium-frequency active search
Aircraft: 16 fixed-wing or 18 helicopters

Giuseppe Garibaldi, *Harrier II and Sea Kings embarked.* (Marina Militare, Italy)

CVS, Chakri Narubet

Chakri Narubet (911) with two AV-8S Matadors on deck. (Bazán)

APART FROM INDIA, Thailand is currently the only Far East navy to operate an aircraft carrier. Plans for such a vessel dated back to the 1980s, and Bremer Vulcan in Germany was initially awarded a contract for a small 7,800-ton carrier. However, this contract was cancelled in 1991 and agreement was reached in 1992 with the Spanish Bazán yard to build a ship similar in layout to the *Príncipe de Asturias*, although only two thirds the displacement of the Spanish ship. Despite this, the flightdeck is only slightly shorter and the Thai carrier has twin MTU diesels as well as the LM2500 gas turbines for economic cruising.

Laid down in July 1994, the *Chakri Narubet* was launched in January 1996 and commissioned on 27 March 1997. Trials and operational work-up were carried out in Spanish waters and the ship did not reach Thailand until August 1997. To save costs the ship was delivered without some armament and other equipment, the intention being to upgrade to the required standard at a later date. As part of the agreement to have the ship built in Spain, the Thai Navy received seven AV-8S Matadors (Harrier), plus two two-seater TAV-8S which had previously flown with the Spanish Navy but were surplus to requirements when Spain took delivery of new AV-8B Harrier Plus aircraft. The Matadors are flown by 301 Squadron while 302 Squadron operates seven S-70B Seahawk helicopters. A typical air group comprises six AV-8S Matador and six Seahawk multi-mission helicopters. However, since entering service the ship has mostly operated as a helicopter carrier with the Harriers embarking for short periods only, due to problems with serviceability caused by a lack of spare parts. Nevertheless, the possession of this ship gives the Thai Navy a considerable advantage over others in the area.

SPECIFICATION

Type: CVS
Class: Chakri Narubet
Displacement: 11,485 tons full load
Length: oa 599.1ft (182.6m), wl 538.4ft (164.1m), flightdeck 572.8ft (174.6m)
Beam: oa 100.1ft (30.5m), wl 73.8ft (22.5m)
Draught: 20.3ft (6.2m)
Machinery: CODOG; 2 GE LM2500 gas turbines, 44,250hp; 2 MTU 16V 1163 TB83 diesels, 11,780 hp; 2 shafts, cp propellers
Speed & Range: 26kt (16kt diesels); 10,000 miles (16,090km) at 12kt
Complement: 455 + 146 air group
Missiles: 1 Mk.41 eight-cell VLS for Sea Sparrow SAM; 3 sextuple launchers, Mistral short-range SAM
Guns: 4 20mm Vulcan/Phalanx CIWS; 2 30mm guns (to be fitted when available)
ASW & USW: nil
Sensors: radar: Hughes SPS-52C air search, SPS-64 surface search, Signaal SATIR fire control, Kelvin Hughes navigation and aircraft control; sonar: hull-mounted medium-frequency active search
Aircraft: 6 fixed-wing, 6 helicopters

SUBMARINES

These currently fall into three main categories of which the most powerful are the strategic submarines (SSBN) carrying long-range ballistic missiles armed with nuclear warheads. It is almost impossible to imagine the destructive power carried by just one of these vessels, whose crews literally have the fate of the world in their hands. Both the United States and Russia maintain large fleets of strategic submarines, while Britain and France both deploy a significant number. A fifth entrant to this exclusive club is China, which has the missile technology but has so far only sent one or two missile-carrying submarines to sea, although the potential for further construction is substantial. However, the status of the ballistic missile as a major strategic weapon is now subject to competition as the submarine-launched cruise missile becomes increasingly more sophisticated and ballistic missile numbers are progressively reduced under the various strategic arms reduction treaties (START). The US Navy is now building the Virginia class of cruise-missile-armed nuclear-powered submarines which are expected to enter service in 2004.

The second group of submarines is the nuclear-powered attack submarine (SSN) whose main role is the location and destruction of enemy underwater forces. However, they are also very effective against surface warships, using either modern sophisticated guided torpedoes such as the British Spearfish or the American Mk.48 ADCAP, or submarine-launched anti-ship missiles with ranges of up to 100 miles (160km). Many of these boats have been adapted to launch cruise missiles for use against land targets so that altogether they have a substantial offensive capability, made even more effective by the difficulty of hunting and successfully attacking them. In addition to the US and Russian navies, SSNs are also operated by Britain, France, and China.

Finally there are the conventional diesel-powered submarines (SSK) which continue to be developed and which still offer some advantages over the larger nuclear-powered boats, cost being one of the most significant. Although smaller in size, most of them are equipped with sophisticated sonar equipment and armed with torpedoes and anti-ship missiles. They are very quiet and better suited to shallow-water operations in littoral areas than their larger nuclear-powered counterparts. SSKs are operated by a large number of navies as they provide a cost-effective way of building up an effective naval presence. As such they form a threat of which the larger navies must take note. An exciting development now being incorporated into some of the latest SSK projects such as the Swedish A19 and German Type 212 is the use of an air independent propulsion system (AIP) to supplement conventional diesels. This allows the submarine to operate continuously underwater for periods of up to two or three weeks.

SSBN, Typhoon/Akula (Type 941)

THESE ARE THE LARGEST submarines ever built by a considerable margin and the inspiration for the well-known Tom Clancy novel *The Hunt for Red October*. The construction features an unusual twin-pressure hull configuration with a single outer hull casing accounting for the massive beam of 80.7ft (24.6m) – wider than some aircraft carriers. At least six of these massive boats were planned and the first was laid down in 1975 for completion in 1981, although some of the later boats were completed in less than three years. All were built at the Sererodvinsk Shipyard, and the last commissioned in 1989.

Unusually, the launch tubes for the SS-N-20 Sturgeon missiles are carried in the hull forward of the sail. Ten tubes are installed in each hull and the missiles have a range of 5,160 miles (8,300km), each carrying 10 MIRV with a 200-kiloton nuclear warhead. Each of the 23.6ft (7.2m) diameter hulls also accommodates its own nuclear powerplant plus separate electric motors for emergency and silent running. The diving depth is 1,000ft (300m) and the sail and hull are strengthened for operations under the Arctic ice field. Interesting and powerful as these boats are, they are expensive to maintain and man, and four have already been laid up or decommissioned. It is likely that the remaining vessels will be withdrawn from service in the near future.

Typhoon class Type 941 SSBN.
(via Naval Technology)

SPECIFICATION

Type: SSBN
Class: Typhoon/Akula (Type 941)
Displacement: 18,500 tons surface, 26,500 tons dived
Length: 562.7ft (171.5m)
Beam: 80.7ft (24.6m)
Draught: 42.7ft (13m)
Machinery: nuclear; 2 VM-5 PWR type reactors, 380MW; 2 GT3A turbines, 81,600hp; 2 emergency motors; 2 shafts, shrouded propellers; 2 manoeuvring thrusters, 2,860hp
Speed & Range: 25kt dived
Complement: 175
Missiles: 20 SS-N-20 Sturgeon SLBMs, each carrying a 10 MIRV nuclear warhead; SA-N-8 SAM (for surface use)
Guns: nil
ASW & USW: 6 21in (553mm) torpedo tubes, various torpedo types including nuclear-tipped; SS-N-15 Starfish long-range A/S missile-carrying nuclear warhead or Type 40 torpedo
Sensors: radar: Snoop Par surface search; sonar: Shark Gill hull-mounted active/passive search and attack; Shark Rib passive flank array; Mouse Roar hull-mounted high-frequency active attack; Pelamida passive towed array
Aircraft: nil

SSBN, Ohio

T HESE 18 STRATEGIC MISSILE SUBMARINES (SSBN-726–743) form the backbone of the US nuclear deterrent and have completely replaced the older Poseidon-armed Franklin and Madison classes. They are characterised by the very long hull required to carry the 24 Trident missile launch tubes, and consequently the sail is set well forward. The first of class, USS Ohio (SSBN-726), was laid down in April 1976, launched in April 1979 and commissioned on 11 November 1981. The building programme continued at the rate of one a year until the last, USS Louisiana (SSBN-743), commissioned in 1997.

In service the nuclear reactors have an expected life of 15 years without refuelling and the hull has a safe diving depth of 800ft (250m) – not as great as most Russian boats. The first eight boats were armed with the 4,600-mile (7,400-km) range Trident I (C4) SLBM, and the Trident II (D5) with a range of 6,500 miles (10,460km) was introduced in the ninth boat, USS Tennessee (SSBN-734), completed in 1988. Four of the early vessels (SSBN-730–733) were being modified from 1998 onwards to take the Trident II, but the first four boats will probably be rebuilt to carry up to 154 non-nuclear-armed Tomahawk land attack and anti-ship cruise missiles. This is to comply with the START II treaty which required the number of nuclear missile armed hulls to be reduced to 14 by 2003.

The US Navy is currently conducting trials with non-nuclear Trident warheads which use GPS and mid-course guidance for precision attacks on land targets. In fact, the Ohio class may in any case be the last US submarines to carry large ballistic missiles as the projected Virginia class, which is expected to enter service around 2004, will be armed entirely with Tomahawk cruise missiles and similar weapons.

Ohio class submarine USS **Alabama** *(SSBN-731). (US Navy)*

USS **Maine** *(SSBN-741). (US Navy)*

SPECIFICATION

Type: SSBN
Class: Ohio
Displacement: 16,600 tons surface, 18,750 tons dived
Length: 560ft (170.7m)
Beam: 42ft (12.8m)
Draught: 36.4ft (11.1m)
Machinery: nuclear; 1 GE S8G PWR reactor, 60,000hp; 1 shaft; 1 auxiliary propulsion motor, 325hp
Speed & Range: 24kt dived
Complement: 155
Missiles: 24 Trident I or Trident II SLBMs with 8 or 12 thermonuclear MIRVs
Guns: nil
ASW & USW: 4 21in (533mm) torpedo tubes, Mk.48 wire-guided torpedoes
Sensors: radar: BPS 15A surface search and navigation; sonar: BQS 6 passive search; BQS 15 high-frequency active close range; BQR 15 passive towed array; BQR 19 active high-frequency (navigation)
Aircraft: nil

SSBN, Vanguard

THE ROYAL NAVY HAS BEEN RESPONSIBLE for Britain's nuclear deterrent since the Resolution class nuclear submarines entered service in 1967 carrying the 2,500-mile (4,000-km) range Polaris missile. In 1980 it was decided to buy the Trident missile from the United States and a new class of submarines designed to carry the Trident II (D5) missile was ordered in 1986. The first of these, HMS Vanguard, was laid down in 1986 and commissioned in 1993. She was followed by Victorious in 1995, Vigilant in 1996 and Vengeance in 1999. All four were built by Vickers Shipbuilding and Engineering (now part of BAE Systems) at Barrow in Furness. The older Polaris boats were withdrawn over the same period, the last to go being HMS Repulse in 1996.

The Trident II missile carried by the Vanguard class has a range of 7,460 miles (12,00km) and can theoretically carry up to 12 MIRVs with 100–120-kiloton nuclear warheads. However, as a result of strategic arms limitation treaties, Britain has agreed to reduce the total number of warheads aboard each submarine to a maximum of 48 (i.e. three per missile) and has also developed low-yield non-strategic warheads which were available from 1996.

The Vanguard class boats are capable of normal submarine operations and are armed with Marconi Spearfish wire-guided torpedoes, although whether such high-value assets could be risked in such a manner is open to question. Despite a deliberate stretching of the original programme timescale, the Trident programme and the associated Vanguard class submarines must be unique among major UK defence projects in that the whole process was completed at less than the original cost estimates, after allowing for inflation.

Below and above right: *HMS* Vanguard, *the first of four SSBNs completed for the Royal Navy. (Royal Navy)*

SPECIFICATION

Type: SSBN
Class: Vanguard
Displacement: 15,900 tons dived
Length: 491.8ft (149.9m)
Beam: 42ft (12.8m)
Draught: 39.4ft (12m)
Machinery: nuclear; 1 Rolls-Royce PWR reactor; 2 GEC turbines, 27,500hp; 1 shaft, pump jet propulsion; 2 auxiliary retractable propulsion motors; 2 turbo generators, 6MW; 2 Paxman diesel alternators, 2,700hp
Speed & Range: 25kt dived
Complement: 135
Missiles: 16 Trident II (D5) three-stage solid fuel SLBMs
Guns: nil
ASW & USW: 4 21in (553mm) torpedo tubes, Marconi Spearfish dual-purpose wire-guided torpedoes
Sensors: radar: Type 1007 navigation; sonar: Type 2054 composite sonar suite comprising Type 2043 hull-mounted active/passive search, Type 2082 passive intercept and ranging, and Type 2046 towed array
Aircraft: nil

SSBN, Le Triomphant

DURING THE 1980s it was originally planned to build six of these submarines to form the backbone of the French seaborne nuclear deterrent forces in the 21st century. *Le Triomphant* was ordered in 1986, but with the break-up of the Soviet Union and the perceived end of the Cold War, together with budgetary constraints, follow-up orders were cut back. Currently there are two boats in service with a third, Le *Vigilant*, due to commission in 2004, and a fourth and last boat *Le Terrible*, was ordered in 2000 for service in 2008.

All four are built by DCN at Cherbourg and are entirely French in concept and construction. This includes the Aérospatiale M45/TN75 ballistic missiles which have a range of 3,300 miles (5,300km), carrying six MIRVs each with a 150-kiloton thermonuclear warhead. The fourth boat will carry the improved M51/TN75 with range increased to 5,000 miles (8,000km), and this version will subsequently equip the earlier boats. For more conventional warfare, the Le Triomphant class carries a mix of 18 Exocet SSM or ECAN L5 Mod 3 dual-purpose torpedoes, with the Exocets being launched through the torpedo tubes.

Le Téméraire, *Le Triomphant class SSBN*. (Marine Nationale, *France*)

The hull is built of HLES high elasticity steel and is capable of diving safely to 1,650ft (500m).

Le Triomphant was launched in July 1993 and commenced a long period of trials which included live firings of the M45 missile in 1994. These took some time, and she did not formally commission until May 1997 after a post-trial refit. The second boat, *Le Téméraire*, commissioned in December 1999.

Le Téméraire, *Le Triomphant class SSBN*. (Marine Nationale, *France*)

SPECIFICATION

Type: SSBN
Class: Le Triomphant
Displacement: 12,640 tons surface, 14,335 tons dived
Length: 453ft (138m)
Beam: hull 41ft (12.5m)
Draught: 41ft (12.5m)
Machinery: nuclear, turbo electric; 1 PWR Type K15 reactor, 150MW; 2 turbo alternators, 1 motor, 41,500hp; diesel electric auxiliary propulsion; 2 SEMT-Pielstick 8 PA4 V200 SM diesels, emergency motor; 1 shaft, pump jet propulsor
Speed & Range: 25kt dived
Complement: 111
Missiles: 16 Aérospatiale M45/TN75 three-stage solid fuel SLBM; Aérospatiale SM39 Exocet SSM
Guns: nil
ASW & USW: 4 21in (553mm) torpedo tubes, ECAN L5 A/S torpedoes
Sensors: radar: Dassault I-band search; sonar: Thompson Sintra DMUX 80 multi-function passive; VLF towed array
Aircraft: nil

SSBN, Delta (Type 667 BDRM)

THESE LARGE BOATS FORM THE BACKBONE of the Russian nuclear missile force and have been in production since 1969 with the first commissioning in 1972. They were the first Russian ballistic missile submarines to house the missiles within the hull in the manner of contemporary US and British strategic submarines, the previous Golf and Hotel classes only carrying three missiles in launchers installed in the after-section of the extended sail. In fact, even the Deltas have not entirely recessed the missiles and a recognition feature is the extended raised casing covering the 12 or 16 launch tubes stretching aft of the sail.

There have been four distinct variants with no fewer than 18 of the original Delta Is armed with 12 Sawfly two-stage missiles being completed, although the last of them decommissioned in 2000. The Delta II was identical except that the hull was lengthened to accommodate 16 missiles, but only four of this version were built and they also have now been decommissioned. These were followed by 14 Delta IIIs (completed 1975–82) which carried the SS-N-18 Stingray SLBM capable of ranges up to 5,000 miles (8,000km). This version could be distinguished by a much higher casing which rose to just below the top of the sail in order to accommodate the longer SS-N-18 missiles.

Most of the Delta IIIs have been decommissioned since 1996 and fewer than half a dozen remain in service. The final version was the Delta IV, of which seven were completed between 1985 and 1992, and all of these are currently in service, armed with the SS-N-23 Skiff three-stage SLBM with a range of 5,188 miles (8,300km), each carrying up to 10 MIRVs with 100-kiloton nuclear warheads. The data given in the box applies to the Delta IV class.

A view of a Delta IV SSBN, emphasising the bulk of the SLBM silo abaft the sail. (via Naval Technology)

SPECIFICATION

Type: SSBN
Class: Delta (Type 667)
Displacement: 10,800 tons surface, 13,500 tons dived
Length: 544.6ft (166m)
Beam: 39.4ft (12m)
Draught: 28.5ft (8.7m)
Machinery: nuclear; 2 VM-4 PWR reactors, 180MW; 2 GT3A-365 turbines, 37,400hp; 2 emergency motors, 612hp; 2 shafts
Speed & Range: 24kt dived, 14kt surface
Complement: 135
Missiles: 16 vertical launch tubes, SS-N-23 long-range ballistic missiles with 4–10 MIRV nuclear warheads
Guns: nil
ASW & USW: 4 21in (533mm) torpedo tubes, various torpedoes; SS-N-15 Starfish anti-submarine missile
Sensors: radar: Snoop Tray surface search; sonar: Shark Gill hull-mounted active/passive search and attack; Shark Hide passive flank array; Mouse Roar hull-mounted high-frequency attack; Pelamida passive towed array
Aircraft: nil

SSBN, L'Inflexible (M4)

F RANCE'S FIRST NUCLEAR-POWERED strategic missile-armed submarines were the four Le Redoutable class boats commissioned between 1973 and 1980. These were joined in 1985 by a single improved version, L'Inflexible, which introduced the new M4 SLBM in place of the earlier M20, although most of the Le Redoutable class boats were subsequently refitted to carry the new missile between 1985 and 1992. Other improvements included the fitting of DSUX 21 sonar and a modification of the bow casing. The exception was Le Redoutable herself, decommissioned in 1991. With the advent of the newer and larger Le Triomphant class, most of the older boats have also now been retired, leaving only L'Indomptable to remain in service until 2004, while the later L'Inflexible will not decommission until 2006.

L'Inflexible class SSBN.
(Marine Nationale, France)

These boats carry the Aérospatiale M4/TN70 or TN71 submarine-launched ballistic missile with a range of 3,300 miles (5,300km), carrying six MIRVs each armed with a 150-kiloton nuclear warhead. A mix of Exocet SSM and conventional torpedoes is also carried. Diving depth is 650ft (200m). Although these boats are nuclear-powered and theoretically have an unlimited range, they can also cover up to 5,000 miles (8,000km) at four knots using the diesel electric auxiliary propulsion system. This ensures that the submarine can return safely to port in the event of a shutdown of the nuclear powerplant.

L'Inflexible class SSBN.
(Marine Nationale, France)

SPECIFICATION

Type: SSBN
Class: L'Inflexible (M4)
Displacement: 8,080 tons surface, 8,920 tons dived
Length: 422.1ft (128.7m)
Beam: 34.8ft (10.6m)
Draught: 32.8ft (10m)
Machinery: nuclear, turbo electric; 1 PWR reactor; 2 turbo alternators; 1 Jeumont Schneider motor, 16,000hp; diesel electric auxiliary propulsion – 2 SEMT-Pielstick/Jeumont Schneider 8 PA4V 185SMs, 1.5MW; 1 emergency motor; single shaft
Speed & Range: 25kt dived, 20kt surface
Complement: 130
Missiles: 16 Aérospatiale M4/TN70 three-stage solid fuel SLBMs; Aérospatiale SM39 Exocet SSM
Guns: nil
ASW & USW: 4 21in (533mm) torpedo tubes, ECLAN L5 A/S torpedoes
Sensors: radar: Thompson DRUA-33 navigation; sonar: Thompson Sintra DSUX 21 multi-function passive; DUUX 5 passive ranging and intercept; DSUV 61 towed array
Aircraft: nil

SSGN, Oscar (Type 949A)

THESE MONSTER SUBMARINES are characterised by an extremely wide hull casing. In fact, the pressure hull is only 28ft (8.5m) in diameter, but this is more than doubled by the addition of the SS-N-19 missile banks on either beam, 12 being carried on each side. These are angled forward at 40° with a sliding hatch covering each pair. The SS-N-19 Shipwreck has a range of up to 300 miles (480km) and is a submarine-launched version of the same missile which arms the Kirov class battlecruisers.

Only two Type 949 Oscar Is were built, entering service in 1982–83, but both are now de-commissioned. The Oscar II was basically similar except the hull was lengthened by 26ft (8m), and 12 of these were laid down for completion between 1988 and 2000, although the last to be launched, *Belgorod*, may not be completed. Despite their great size, they are also employed in the ASW role, carrying a comprehensive sonar suite including a passive towed array. The SS-N-15 Starfish missile has a range of 28 miles (45km) while the larger SS-N-16 Stallion is effective up to 62 miles (100km). Both of these missiles can carry either a nuclear warhead or a Type 40 torpedo and both are launched via the torpedo tubes, the SS-N-16 from the larger 26in (660mm) tubes. A total of 28 missiles and torpedoes can be carried.

Oscar class SSN underway.
(via Naval Technology)

One of these submarines was lost in the Barents Sea on 12 August 2000 following a massive internal explosion. A total of 118 lives were lost despite frantic efforts to rescue any survivors. All Oscar IIs have since been withdrawn from service until the cause of the accident can be established.

SPECIFICATION

Type: SSGN
Class: Oscar (Type 949)
Displacement: 13,900 tons surface, 18,300 tons dived
Length: 505.2ft (154m)
Beam: 59.7ft (18.2m)
Draught: 29.5ft (9m)
Machinery: nuclear; 2 VM-5 PWR reactors, 380MW; 2 GT-3A turbines, 98,000hp; 2 shafts; 2 spinners
Speed & Range: 28kt dived
Complement: 107
Missiles: 24 SS-N-19 Shipwreck long-range SSMs, 12 fixed launch tubes on either beam
Guns: nil
ASW & USW: 2 26in (660mm) and 4 21in (533mm) torpedo tubes, various torpedoes – SS-N-15 A/S missile launched from 21in (533mm) torpedo tubes, SS-N-16 Stallion long-range A/S missile launched from 26in (660mm) tubes
Sensors: radar: Snoop Pair or Snoop Half surface search; sonar: Shark Gill hull-mounted search and attack; Shark Rib passive flank array; Mouse Roar hull-mounted high-frequency active attack; Pelamida passive towed array
Aircraft: nil

Oscar class SSN, general arrangement drawing.
(via Naval Technology)

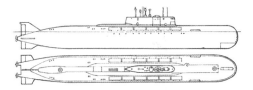

UNITED STATES

SSN, Seawolf

INTENDED AS A BIGGER, FASTER AND BETTER armed follow-on to the Los Angeles class, the Seawolf programme has been hit by the end of the Cold War and a reduction in funding so that only two boats have been completed (*Seawolf*, SSN-21, in 1997 and *Connecticut*, SSN-22, in 1998), while one further boat (*Jimmy Carter*, SSN-23) will commission at the end of 2001. One reason for the cutback was the fact that each boat cost around $2 billion and such expense could not be justified despite a substantial performance improvement over the Los Angeles class. In particular, Seawolfs are considerably quieter and are reported to be virtually silent at up to 20kt. The hull has been tested to a depth of 2,000ft (600m), much deeper than any other operational US submarine and comparable with the best achieved by the Russians.

Internally, the Seawolfs can carry a total of 50 tube-launched missiles and torpedoes launched from the eight 26in (660mm) torpedo tubes. Apart from Tomahawk and Harpoon missiles, the Mk.48 ADCAP torpedo is also carried and this has a range of up to 31 miles (50km) at speeds of up to 40kt, or shorter ranges at 55kt. As an alternative to the normal weapon load, a total of 100 mines can be carried. Externally, they are easily recognised on the surface by virtue of an unusual forward sweep on the leading edge of the fin. As with the later Los Angeles class, the hydroplanes are retractable and the hull is strengthened to allow for operations under the ice field.

Future SSN production will centre on the Virginia class which is expected to be at least 30% cheaper while still retaining the acoustic characteristics of the SSN-21 class, although it will be slower and not able to dive so deep or be suited to under-ice operations. However, it will carry a comprehensive weapons outfit including surface-to-surface missiles and Mk.48 torpedoes, as well as Tomahawk SLCMs launched from 12 VLS tubes. Up to 30 Virginia class boats may be built if the US Navy's SSN force is to be maintained at a minimum of 50 hulls over the next two or three decades.

***USS** Seawolf, SSN-21. (US Navy)*

SPECIFICATION

Type: SSN
Class: Seawolf (SSN-21)
Displacement: 8,060 tons surface, 9,142 tons dived
Length: 353ft (107.6m)
Beam: 42.3ft (12.9m)
Draught: 35.8ft (10.9m)
Machinery: nuclear; 1 Westinghouse S6W PWR reactor, 2 turbines, 45,000hp; 1 shaft, pump jet propulsor; 1 secondary propulsion motor
Speed & Range: 39kt dived
Complement: 134
Missiles: Tomahawk TLAM-N land attack cruise missiles with nuclear warheads; Tomahawk TLAM-C/D with conventional warheads; Tomahawk TASM anti-ship cruise missiles (option)
Guns: nil
ASW & USW: 8 26in (660mm) torpedo tubes, Mk.48 ADCAP wire-guided torpedoes
Sensors: radar: BPS 16 navigation; sonar: BQQ 5D comprising bow-mounted active/passive and flank-mounted passive arrays; TB16 and TB29 towed arrays
Aircraft: nil

SSN, Akula (Type 971)

THESE ARE AMONG THE MOST EFFECTIVE of the Russian nuclear-powered attack submarines and are the direct successors of the earlier Victor classes, although unlikely to be built in anything like the same numbers. Capable of diving to almost 1,500ft (450m), they are extremely quiet in operation and therefore difficult to locate and track; characterised by an extremely broad and streamlined hull, unlike any submarine built for western navies, some Russian sources have suggested that they can go to twice that depth. As with other Russian submarines, they have been built in more than one version and there are currently eight of the original 12 Akulas in service. The first commissioned in 1985 and the others followed at intervals up to 1995.

Akula means 'Shark' in Russian, and these boats are named after fish and animals including the dolphin, narwhal, leopard, tiger and dragon. They are heavily armed: the SS-N-21 Sampson land attack cruise missiles, equivalent to the US Tomahawk, have a range of 1,860 miles (3,000km) at Mach 0.7 carrying a 200-kiloton nuclear warhead; in addition to ASW missiles and torpedoes (a total of 40 such weapons can be carried in any combination), the Akulas are one of the few submarines to carry any form of air defence in the form of Strela short-range surface-to-air missiles.

Despite being relatively modern, four Akulas have been laid up since 1996 and production of the lengthened Akula IIs has slowed down to a trickle. One was completed in 1995, a second in mid 2000, but a third has been considerably delayed and may not be completed.

Akula class (Type 971) SSN.
(RAF Kinloss/MoD)

SPECIFICATION

Type: SSN

Class: Akula (Type 971)

Displacement: 7,500 tons surface, 9,100 tons dived

Length: 360.1ft (110m)

Beam: 45.9ft (14m)

Draught: 34.1ft (10.4m)

Machinery: nuclear; 1 VM-5 PWR reactor, 190MW; 2 GT3A turbines, 47,600hp; 2 emergency motors, 750hp; 1 shaft

Speed & Range: 28kt dived

Complement: 62

Missiles: SS-N-21 Sampson land attack cruise missiles; SS-N-27 long-range SA-N-5 or 8 very short-range SAMs; surface use, portable launchers; SS-N-15 Starfish A/S missile

Guns: nil

ASW & USW: 4 (or 10) 21in (533mm) torpedo tubes, various torpedoes; 4 25.6in (650mm) torpedo tubes, Type 65 long-range torpedoes

Sensors: radar: Snoop Pair or Snoop Half, surface search; sonar: Shark Gill hull-mounted active/passive search and attack; Mouse Roar hull-mounted high-frequency active attack; Skat 3 passive towed array

Aircraft: nil

UNITED STATES
SSN, Los Angeles

USS San Francisco
(SSN-711),
Los Angeles class SSN.
(US Navy)

THIS IS A LARGE CLASS CURRENTLY comprising no fewer than 51 boats, although a total of 62 was built originally. The first commissioned in 1976 and production continued at the rate of two or three a year until the last, USS *Cheyenne* (SSN-773), entered service in 1996. The first batch was numbers SSN-688 to SSN-725, while subsequent boats were numbered from SSN-750 onwards. A number of the earlier boats have been paid off, but the US Navy is reluctant to take more out of service until the new Virginia class boats begin to enter service around 2004. However, the 1997 Defence Review determined that SSN numbers should be reduced to 50 by 2003 and, allowing for the three Seawolf class boats, this would mean that a further four Los Angeles class boats will have to go by that date.

The Tomahawk and Harpoon missiles can be fired from the torpedo tubes and the normal weapons outfit comprises a mix of 26 torpedoes and missiles. Nuclear warheads are available, but are not normally embarked. From the USS *Providence*, SSN-719, onwards 12 vertical launch tubes are installed outside the forward pressure hull to allow extra Tomahawk missiles to be carried. The land attack version of the Tomahawk has a maximum range of 1,550 miles (2,500km) and the anti-ship version (TASM) is also carried, which can engage targets to a range of 280 miles (450km).

The USS *San Juan* (SSN-751), which commissioned in 1988, introduced a number of improvements aimed at reducing the acoustic signature. These included acoustic tiling similar to that seen in the British SSNs and the forward hydroplanes were moved from their previous position on the sail to the forward hull, where they can be retracted for surfacing through ice.

Several Los Angeles class boats took part in the Gulf War, firing Tomahawk missiles against targets in Iraq from positions in the eastern Mediterranean and the Gulf.

SPECIFICATION

Type: SSN
Class: Los Angeles
Displacement: 6,082 tons surface, 6,927 tons dived
Length: 362ft (110.3m)
Beam: 33ft (10.1m)
Draught: 32.3ft (9.9m)
Machinery: nuclear; 1 GE S6G PWR reactor; 2 turbines, 35,000hp; 1 shaft; 1 auxiliary propulsion motor, 325hp
Speed & Range: 32kt dived
Complement: 133
Missiles: Tomahawk TLAM-N land attack cruise missile; Tomahawk TASM long-range anti-ship missile; Boeing Harpoon SSM
Guns: nil
ASW & USW: 4 21in (533mm) torpedo tubes, Mk.48 ADCAP wire-guided long-range torpedoes
Sensors: radar: BPS15H surface search and navigation; sonar: BQQ 5D/E active/passive low-frequency search and attack; BQG 5D passive flank array; passive towed array (various equipment); BQS 15 close-range high-frequency active; MIDAS – active high-frequency mine and ice detection and avoidance system
Aircraft: nil

SSN, Victor (Type 671RTM)

APPROXIMATELY SEVEN VICTOR III CLASS boats are currently operational with the Russian Navy, the only survivors of a total of 48 boats built from 1968 until 1993 in three distinct variants. By Russian standards they are relatively small but they are nevertheless well armed and equipped. The original Type 671 Victor I displaced 4,300 tons on the surface and could dive to 1,300 ft (400m); 15 were completed between 1968 and 1975. A further Type 671PT Victor IIs entered service between 1972 and 1978 and these had a hull lengthened by 16ft (5m) and displacement rose to 4,500 tons. The current Type 671PTM Victor II had a further section added to the hull, increasing the length to 345ft (105m) and displacement to 4,900 tons, and could be distinguished visually by a large streamlined pod mounted above the stern which contained the towed array sonar system. One boat was modified to incorporate a trials launch system in front of the sail for the SS-N-21 missiles, which are normally fired from the forward torpedo tubes, and this boat is sometimes referred to as a Victor IV (Type 671RTMK).

The last Victor IIIs built utilised eight-bladed propellers and are much quieter than their predecessors, and are almost comparable to the US SSNs in this respect. A total of 26 Victor IIIs were built, commissioning between 1978 and 1991, but today no more than seven are active and all Victor I and IIs have been laid up or scrapped. In the long term the remaining Victors will be replaced by the newer Akula and Sierra classes, although construction of the latter appears to have ceased some time ago.

Above and below: *Victor III class Type 671RTM SSN. (RAF Kinloss/MoD)*

SPECIFICATION

Type: SSN
Class: Victor (Type 671RTM)
Displacement: 4,850 tons surface, 6,300 tons dived
Length: 351.1ft (107m)
Beam: 34.8ft (10.6m)
Draught: 24.3ft (7.4m)
Machinery: nuclear; 2 VM-4 PWR reactors, 150MW; 2 turbines, 31,000hp; 1 shaft; 2 spinners
Speed & Range: 30kt dived
Complement: 98
Missiles: SS-N-21 Sampson long-range SLCM
Guns: nil
ASW & USW: 2 26in (660mm) and 4 21in (553mm) torpedo tubes, various torpedoes; SS-N-15 Starfish A/S missile launched from 21in (533mm) torpedo tubes; SS-N-16 Stallion long-range A/S missile launched from 26in (660mm) tubes; or 36 mines in lieu of torpedoes
Sensors: radar: Snoop Tray surface search; sonar: Shark Gill hull-mounted search and attack; Shark Rib passive flank array; Mouse Roar hull-mounted high-frequency active attack; Scat 3 passive towed array
Aircraft: nil

UNITED KINGDOM
SSN, Trafalgar

Trafalgar class SSN. (Royal Navy)

THE BRITISH NUCLEAR-POWERED SUBMARINE programme began with HMS *Dreadnought*, which was completed in 1963. She was followed by the five boats of the Valiant class, and all six had been retired by 1991. Their successors were the six Swiftsure class boats completed between 1974 and 1981 of which five remain in service (*Swiftsure* decommissioned in 1992). Displacing 4,400 tons standard, they have been constantly updated in periodic refits, and *Splendid* was the first British submarine to fire the Tomahawk SLCM, in October 1998. However, she is due to be retired in 2003, and *Spartan* will follow in 2006.

The Swiftsure design was basically repeated with improvements and modifications and named the Trafalgar class. The name ship was laid down in 1979 and commissioned in 1993. She was followed by *Turbulent* (1984), *Tireless* (1984), *Torbay* (1987), *Trenchant* (1989), *Talent* (1990) and *Triumph* in 1991. These are slightly larger than the Swiftsure class but carry a similar armament including Harpoon anti-ship missiles, Tomahawk cruise missiles and Spearfish long-range torpedoes. A prominent feature of both Swiftsure and Trafalgar class submarines is the coating of the hull with anechoic tiles to reduce reflections from active sonars. Unfortunately these have a tendency to come adrift over a period of time and it is rare to see one of these boats without several tiles missing.

All Trafalgar class boats are being progressively updated as they come in for refit and refuelling, and this includes the fitting of Type 2076 hull-mounted active/passive sonar, SMCS (submarine command system) and Tomahawk capability. Diving depth is quoted officially as 1,000ft (300m) but is probably greater than that.

The next nuclear-powered attack submarines for the Royal Navy will be the Acute class, closely based on the Trafalgar class, and the first boat is due to enter service in 2005, with *Ambush* and *Artful* to follow in 2007 and 2008.

SPECIFICATION

Type: SSN
Class: Trafalgar
Displacement: 4,740 tons surface, 5,208 tons dived
Length: 280.1ft (85.4m)
Beam: 32.1ft (9.8m)
Draught: 31.2ft (9.5m)
Machinery: nuclear; 1 Rolls-Royce PWR reactor; 2 GEC turbines, 15,000hp; 1 shaft, pump jet propulsor; 2 turbo generators, 3.2MW; 2 Paxman diesel alternators, 2,800hp; 1 motor for emergency drive; 1 auxiliary retractable propeller
Speed & Range: 32kt dived
Complement: 130
Missiles: Hughes Tomahawk Block III submarine launched cruise missile (SLCM); Boeing UGM-84B Sub Harpoon Block 1C SSM
Guns: nil
ASW & USW: 5 21in (533mm) torpedo tubes, Marconi Spearfish or Tigerfish Mk.24 dual-purpose wire-guided torpedoes
Sensors: radar: Type 1007 navigation; sonar: Type 2020 or 2074 or 2076 hull-mounted low-frequency active/passive search and attack; Type 2007AC or Type 2072 hull-mounted passive flank array; Type 2046 passive towed array; Type 2019 or Type 2082 passive intercept and ranging; Type 2077 short-range active classification
Aircraft: nil

SSN/SSG/SSBN, Han, Song and Xia

A Han class Type 091 nuclear-powered attack submarine of the People's Liberation Army Navy. (US Department of Defense)

The Han class of five nuclear-powered attack submarines (hull nos. 401 to 405) was completed between 1974 and 1990 at the Huludao shipyard. The data box relates to the last three boats which were some 26ft (8m) longer as a result of experience with the first two. No.401 was laid down in 1967 and did not commission until 1974, although even then problems with the nuclear powerplant (China's first at sea) meant that she was not fully operational until the early 1980s. Both of the first two vessels underwent major refits before returning to service in the mid-1990s and this may have been to incorporate modifications applied to the second batch of three boats, which commissioned between 1984 and 1990. In most cases the original Russian sonar and ESM equipment has been replaced by French-designed equipment including the DUUX-5 passive ranging and intercept sonar.

Having gained experience of operating nuclear-powered hunter-killer submarines, the PLAN is planning construction of a new class of Type 093 submarines based on the Russian Victor class. Some work has already been done and the first boat should be launched at the Huludao shipyard in 2003 and a second some two years later. At around 6,000 tons

(dived) these will be larger than the Han Class but few other details are yet available. The PLAN is undoubtedly intent on building up a substantial nuclear-powered submarine fleet but progress is severely limited by the need to acquire and apply the necessary technical expertise. However there should be no doubt that this will be done.

China also operates a substantial fleet of Ming class diesel-powered submarines although most of these are based on the the Russian Romeo class, examples of which were built under licence between 1962 and 1987, while four Kilo class boats were acquired directly from Russia between 1995 and 1999.

The first indigenous design for a modern diesel-powered attack submarine is the Song class of which the first, hull number 320, was laid down at Wuhan shipyard in 1991 and launched in 1994. Sea trials commenced in August 1995 and she was finally commissioned in 1999. At least two other boats of this class are known to be under construction and should commission in 2001. Others may also be planned. Apart from torpedoes, the main offensive armament is the indigenous YJ 8-2 surface-to-surface missile developed from the surface-launched C801.

This has a range of 25 miles (40km) at Mach 0.9 and carries a 365lb (165kg) warhead.

On the surface, the Song class boats are easily recognised by the distinctive sail structure which has the bridge set forward below a streamlined structure housing the masts and periscopes, giving a distinct stepped effect. A spherical bow casing houses the medium-frequency sonar array which is believed to be of French design although probably manufactured in China. The Song class boats displace 1,700 tons on the surface (2,500 tons dived). Some 246ft (74.9m) long, they are powered by four MTU diesels driving electric motors connected to a single shaft, giving an underwater speed of 22 knots.

Although the Chinese surface fleet is expanding rapidly, the establishment of a strategic missile-armed submarine force has progressed much more slowly. Using Russian-supplied plans, a conventionally powered Golf class submarine carrying a single JL-1 or 2 missile in a casing aft of the conning tower was launched as long ago as 1964 and remains in service today as a trials vessel. It was used for the first test firings of the JL-1 (Ju-Lang 1) missile from a submarine in 1982. The nuclear-powered Xia class dates back to the early 1980s and it is believed that two were laid down although one was subsequently lost in an accident in 1985. The *Xia* therefore remains as China's only fully operational strategic missile submarine, having commissioned in 1987 and carried out the first successful missile firing trials in 1988. The design is based on that of the Han class nuclear-powered attack submarines but with the hull extended to accommodate the 12 vertical launch tubes for the ballistic missiles which have a range of 1,100 miles (1,800km) and carry a single 250-kiloton nuclear warhead. The *Xia* underwent a major refit in 1998/99 and is now believed to carry improved JL-1A missiles with a greater range. A new design, designated Type 094, is currently under development and four of these may be built with work due to start in 2000, although this will depend on further development of the JL-2 missile with a two-megaton warhead.

SPECIFICATION

Type: SSN
Class: Han (Type 091)
Displacement: 4,500 tons surface, 5,550 tons dived
Length: First pair 321.5ft (98m), others 347.8ft (106m).
Beam: 32.8ft (10m)
Draught: 24.2ft (7.4m)
Machinery: nuclear; 1 PWR reactor, 90MW; turbo electric drive, 1 shaft
Speed & Range: 25kt dived
Complement: 75
Missiles: YJ 8-2 (C-801) medium-range SSM (launched from torpedo tubes)
Guns: nil
ASW & USW: 6 21in (533mm) torpedo tubes, Yu-1 or Yu-3 active/passive homing torpedoes
Sensors: radar: Snoop Tray surface search; sonar: Trout Cheek medium-frequency active/passive search and attack; DUUX-5 passive ranging and intercept
Aircraft: nil

SPECIFICATION

Type: SSBN
Class: Xia
Displacement: 6,500 tons dived
Length: 393.6ft (120m)
Beam: 33ft (10m)
Draught: 26.2ft (8m)
Machinery: nuclear; 1 PWR reactor, 90MW; turbo electric drive, 1 shaft
Speed & Range: 22kt dived
Complement: 140
Missiles: 12 JL-1 intermediate-range SLBMs with single nuclear warhead
Guns: nil
ASW & USW: 6 21in (533mm) torpedo tubes, Yu-3 active/passive homing torpedoes
Sensors: radar: Snoop Tray surface search; sonar: Trout Cheek medium-frequency active/passive search and attack
Aircraft: nil

SSN, Rubis Améthyste

Rubis *(S601)*. *(Marine Nationale, France)*

THE *RUBIS* WAS LAID DOWN IN 1976, originally as the lead boat for a class of four nuclear-powered attack submarines (*Rubis, Saphir, Casabianca, Emeraude*). Subsequently a second group of four similar boats was ordered and the first was laid down in 1983. This group was named Améthyste, which was also an acronym for '*Amélioration Tactique Hydrodynamique Silence Transmission Écoute*' (reduced radiated noise transmission). The second boat of this class was *Perle*, but the last two of this order (*Turquoise, Diamant*) were cancelled due to budgetary problems. Subsequently the four earlier Rubis class boats were modernised to Améthyste standards to create the present class of six boats with identical tactical capabilities, particularly in the ASW role.

The offensive payload is a total of 14 torpedoes and Exocet missiles, or alternatively a load of up to 32 FG29 mines can be carried. With a surface displacement of only 2,410 tons, these boats are the world's smallest nuclear-powered attack submarines and this is made possible by a substantial reduction in the size and weight of the nuclear powerplant compared to that installed aboard the L'Inflexible class SSBNs. Although the powerplant endurance is unlimited for all practical purposes, the normal maximum time at sea is 45 days, the limiting factor being the stowage of provisions for the crew. The diving depth is 1,000 ft (300m).

The French Navy is currently planning a new class of SSNs under the code-name Project Barracuda. The first of these will be ordered in 2001 and is expected to be completed in 2008. Outline details include a displacement of 4,000 tons and a vertical launch system for surface-to-surface missiles. It is expected that six boats will be built over a period of 12 years to replace the present Améthyste class on a one for one basis.

SPECIFICATION

Type: SSN
Class: Rubis Améthyste
Displacement: 2,410 tons surface, 2,670 tons dived
Length: 241.5ft (73.6m)
Beam: 24.9ft (7.6m)
Draught: 21ft (6.4m)
Machinery: nuclear, turbo electric; 1 PWR CAS48 reactor, 48MW; 2 turbo alternators, 1 motor, 9,500hp; diesel electric auxiliary propulsion, 450kW; 1 emergency motor; 1 shaft
Speed & Range: 25kt
Complement: 68
Missiles: Aérospatiale SM39 Exocet SSM (launched from torpedo tubes)
Guns: nil
ASW & USW: 4 21in (533mm) torpedo tubes, ECAN L5 dual-purpose and ECAN F17 wire-guided torpedoes
Sensors: radar: Kelvin Hughes 1007 navigation; sonar: DMUX 20 multi-function low-frequency passive search; DSUV62C towed passive array
Aircraft: nil

Améthyste *(S605)*. *(Marine Nationale, France)*

AUSTRALIA
SSK, Collins

THIS CLASS OF SIX MODERN diesel electric submarines represented an important step forward for the Australian shipbuilding industry. Their construction followed an international competition to find a suitable design; the Swedish Kockums Type 471 was the winner and sections of the first boat, HMAS *Collins*, were actually prefabricated in Sweden, although the remaining work was carried out by the Australian Submarine Corporation at its Adelaide yard. The lead ship, *Collins*, was laid down in 1980, launched on 28 August 1993 and commissioned on 27 July 1996. She was followed by *Farncomb* (commissioned in January 1998), *Waller* (April 1999) and *Dechaineux* in June 2000. *Sheean* was commissioned in October 2000 and the last boat, *Rankin*, will join the fleet in mid 2001.

Unfortunately this ambitious programme has not been without its problems, particularly in the integration of its various complex command and control systems. In addition these boats are considerably noisier than was expected due to propeller cavitation and vibration of the diesel engines coupled with gearbox problems. Strenuous efforts are being made to overcome these deficiencies but it will be well into the current decade before all six boats are fully operational. When the problems are ironed out, these will be among the most advanced diesel electric submarines in the world.

Shore trials of a Stirling AIP propulsion system have been carried out, and it may be applied at future refits. A prominent feature of the Collins class is the massive bulbous bow casing which houses the French-built Sintra advanced sonar system. Internally, a total of 22 missiles and torpedoes may be carried, or alternatively up to 44 mines.

Collins class SSK, one of six boats built in Australia to a Swedish design.
(RAN Photo)

Collins class SSK showing the stern gear for deploying the towed array sonar.
(RAN Photo)

SPECIFICATION

Type: SSK
Class: Collins
Displacement: 3,050 tons surface, 3,353 tons dived
Length: 255.2ft (77.8m)
Beam: 25.6ft (7.8m)
Draught: 23ft (7m)
Machinery: diesel electric; 3 Hedemora/Garden Island Type V18B/14 diesels, 6,020hp; 3 Jeumont Schneider generators, 4.2MW; Jeumont Schneider motor, 7,344hp; 1 hydraulic motor for emergency propulsion
Speed & Range: 10kt surface, 20kt dived; 11,500 miles (18,500km) at 10kt (surface), 400 miles (645km) at 4kt dived
Complement: 42
Missiles: Boeing Sub Harpoon SSM
Guns: nil
ASW & USW: 6 21in (533mm) torpedo tubes capable of discharging Mk.48 dual-purpose wire-guided torpedoes of Sub Harpoon missiles
Sensors: radar: Kelvin Hughes Type 1007 navigation; sonar: Thompson Sintra Scylla active/passive intercept and ranging; retractable passive towed array
Aircraft: nil

SSK, Oyashio

Oyashio class SSK of the JMSDF.
(JMSDF)

JAPAN HAS NO PLANS TO BUILD nuclear-powered submarines but has consistently developed its conventional diesel electric boats. Currently in service are nine 2,300-ton Yuushio class boats built between 1978 and 1989, and seven similar but slightly enlarged 2,500-ton Harushio class boats (built 1987 to 1997). The current production design is the Oyashio class, to which the boxed data applies. These were ordered in 1993 and the name boat was laid down in January 1994, launched on 15 October 1996 and commissioned on 16 March 1998. She was followed by *Michishio*, commissioned in March 1999, and *Uzushio*, in 2000. Another three are due for completion at yearly intervals from 2001 to 2003.

At 2,700 tons standard displacement, they are again slightly larger than their predecessors but can be distinguished by the tapered fin with hydroplanes mounted halfway up. A continuous straight deck casing is also a departure from the early designs, which featured a more rounded whaleback casing design. Sonar capability is improved by the use of passive flank arrays and the fin is encased in anechoic tiles. Torpedoes are Type 89 wire-guided with a maximum range of 31 miles (50km) and a mix of 20 torpedoes and harpoon missiles may be carried.

Like many navies, the Japanese are experimenting with Stirling cycle AIP systems and such engines may well be incorporated when further boats are ordered. In view of Japan's avowed non-nuclear policy, the acquisition of AIP-equipped submarines would be a great advance as it allows sustained continuous underwater operations.

SPECIFICATION

Type: SSK
Class: Oyashio
Displacement: 2,700 tons surface, 3,000 tons dived
Length: 268ft (81.7m)
Beam: 29.2ft (8.9m)
Draught: 25.9ft (7.9m)
Machinery: diesel electric; 2 Kawasaki 12V25S diesels, 5,520hp; 2 Kawasaki alternators, 3.7MW; 2 Fuji motors, 7,750hp; 1 shaft
Speed & Range: 20kt dived
Complement: 69
Missiles: Boeing Sub Harpoon long-range SSM (launched from torpedo tubes)
Guns: nil
ASW & USW: 6 21in (533mm) torpedo tubes, Type 89 wire-guided anti-ship and Type 80 ASW torpedoes
Sensors: radar: ZPS 6 surface search; sonar: ZQQ 5B/6 hull-mounted active/passive search and attack with passive flank arrays; ZQR 1 passive towed array
Aircraft: nil

SSK, Harushio

Harushio class submarine of JMSDF. (JMSDF)

The first of seven Harushio class diesel electric submarines was laid down in April 1987 and commissioned in November 1990. Five more were completed between 1991 and 1995, while a slightly modified seventh boat, *Asashio* (SS-589), commissioned in March 1997. Although conventionally powered, these submarines are very similar to nuclear boats in appearance with a bulbous hull form, the sail set well forward with and carrying the forward hydroplanes. They are optimised for the ASW role although Sub Harpoon missiles and wire-guided Type 89 torpedoes also bestow a substantial anti-ship capability. *Asashio* has recently been converted to the training role.

The Harushio class boats are the result of a steady evolution of Japanese conventional submarine designs. The first were the 1,850-ton Uzushio class boats of which seven were completed during the 1970s although none of these now remain in service. They were followed by ten boats of the Yuushio class, completed between 1980 and 1989, which displaced 2,200 tons on the surface and were slightly longer than their predecessors. Their operational capabilities included the ability to dive to 900 feet (275m) and they introduced towed array sonars and the Sub Harpoon missile system. All eight remain in service although two, *Setoshio* and *Okishio*, are used for training purposes. The succeeding Harushio class boats (described here) were basically similar to the Yuushio class except that the hull was lengthened by approximately one metre and displacement rose by some 200 tons. Electronics and the sonar systems were improved and the hull was given an anechoic

coating. For all practical purposes the two classes were identical in appearance and also shared the same diesel electric machinery.

SPECIFICATION

Type: SSK
Class: Harushio
Displacement: 2,450 tons surface, 2,750 tons dived
Length: 252.6ft (77m)
Beam: 32.8ft (10m)
Draught: 25.3ft (7.7m)
Machinery: diesel electric; 2 Kawasaki 12V25S diesels, 5,520hp; 2 Kawasaki alternators, 3.7MW; 2 Fuji motors, 7,200hp; 1 shaft
Speed: 20kt dived, 12kt surfaced
Complement: 74
Missiles: Boeing Sub Harpoon long-range SSM (launched from torpedo tubes)
Guns: nil
ASW & USW: Six 21in (533mm) torpedo tubes; Type 89 wire-guided anti-ship and Type 80 ASW torpedoes
Sensors: radar: ZPS 6 surface search; sonar: ZQQ 5B hull-mounted active/passive search and attack; ZQR 1 passive towed array
Aircraft: nil

SSK, Walrus

THE INITIAL CONTRACT FOR THE FIRST two boats was awarded in 1979 with a second pair ordered in 1985. Construction was delayed by design changes including a lengthening of the hull to accommodate larger diesel generators and also by a serious fire aboard *Walrus* while it was being fitted out. Consequently the first to commission was *Zeeleeuw* in 1990, followed by the repaired *Walrus* in 1992. The second pair, *Dolfijn* and *Bruinvis*, were laid down in 1986 and 1988, and completed in 1993 and 1994 respectively.

The basic design of these boats was based on the Zwaardvis class, which has now been retired. The hull dimensions were similar but normal diving depth was increased from 650ft (200m) to 1,000ft (300m) by the use of stronger HT steel. A total of 20 Harpoon missiles or torpedoes can be stowed. The latter may include Mk.48 Mod.4 heavyweight wire-guided torpedoes with a range of 23.5 miles (38km) at 55kt or 31 miles (50km) at 40kt, or Honeywell NT37D wire-guided ASW torpedoes with a range of 12.5 miles (20km). As an alternative, up to 40 mines may be carried instead of the torpedoes and missiles. Designed for ocean operations, the Walrus class boats have an endurance of 60 days at sea.

Bruinvis *(S810)*, one of four Walrus class SSKs. *(D. Hannaford)*

Walrus *(S802)*. Note the cruciform stern planes. *(Netherlands Navy via Mönch Archives)*

SPECIFICATION

Type: SSK
Class: Walrus
Displacement: 2,465 tons surface, 2,800 tons dived
Length: 223.ft (67.7m)
Beam: 27.6ft (8.4m)
Draught: 23ft (7m)
Machinery: diesel electric; 3 SEMT-Pielstick 12 PA4 200VG diesels, 6,300hp; 3 alternators, 2.88MW; 1 Holec motor, 6,910hp; 1 shaft
Speed & Range: 20kt dived; 10,000 miles (16,100km) (13kt at surface)
Complement: 52
Missiles: Boeing Sub Harpoon long-range SSM (launched from torpedo tubes)
Guns: nil
ASW & USW: 4 21in (533mm) torpedo tubes, Mk.48 long-range wire-guided and NT37D wire-guided medium-range torpedoes
Sensors: radar: ZW07 surface search; sonar: TSM 2272 hull-mounted active/passive search and attack; Type 2026 passive towed array; DUUX 5 passive ranging and intercept
Aircraft: nil

RUSSIA
SSK, Kilo (Type 877)

IN PRODUCTION SINCE 1979, approximately 12 boats of this class are currently in service with the Russian Navy out of a total of 24 originally laid down. By modern standards they are relatively basic, but they are sturdily built and straightforward to operate, and certainly an improvement on the older Foxtrot and Tango classes which were built in considerable numbers, although only a few now remain in service.

The Kilos have been built in several versions following the basic Type 877. The 887K has a new fire control system while the 877M has the capability to fire wire-guided USET-80 torpedoes from two of the six 21in (533mm) tubes. The Kilo 4B is a developed version with more powerful diesels, a slower and quieter main propulsion motor and an automated combat information system. This version is not, as yet, available for export, although at least six are in service with the Russian Navy, equally split between the Northern and Pacific fleets. In appearance, the Kilos

Kilo class (Type 877) SSK.
(via Naval Technology)

seem short and stumpy, an impression given by the sail which is very long in proportion to the hull length. For self-defence on the surface, there is provision for shoulder-launched SA-N-8 Gremlin SAMs to be fired from a position at the after end of the sail.

The Kilo class boats have proved popular with other navies and a total of 21 have been exported to Poland, Romania, Algeria, India, Iran and China, providing these countries with a very credible submarine capability.

Loading a torpedo aboard a Kilo class SSK.
(via Naval Technology)

SPECIFICATION

Type: SSK
Class: Kilo (Type 877)
Displacement: 2,325 tons surface, 3,076 tons dived
Length: 238.2ft (72.6m)
Beam: 32.5ft (9.9m)
Draught: 21.7ft (6.6m)
Machinery: diesel electric; 2 Type 4-2DL-42M diesels, 3,650hp; 2 generators, 1 motor, 5,900hp; 2 auxiliary and 1 economic cruise motors
Speed & Range: 17kt dived; 6,000 miles (9,650km) at 7kt (surface)
Complement: 52
Missiles: SA-N-5 or 8 short-range SAMs (surface use, portable launcher)
Guns: nil
ASW & USW: 6 21in (533mm) torpedo tubes, various torpedo types; up to 24 mines may be carried instead of torpedoes
Sensors: radar: Snoop Tray surface search; sonar: Shark Teeth/Shark Fin hull-mounted medium-frequency active/passive search and attack; Mouse Roar hull-mounted high-frequency active attack
Aircraft: nil

SSK, Victoria (Type 2400)

Victoria class SSK (ex-UK Upholder class).
(Fleet Photographic Unit, Royal Navy)

THIS CLASS OF FOUR BOATS was ordered for the British Royal Navy in the 1980s and commissioned as the Upholder class between 1991 and 1993. However, following a controversial decision that the Royal Navy would only operate nuclear-powered submarines, the four boats were laid up in 1994. After several years of negotiation, they were eventually sold to Canada in 1998 for a fraction of their original cost and, following refit and modification at Vickers' Barrow in Furness yard, the first became operational again in 2000. Originally named *Upholder*, *Unseen*, *Ursula* and *Unicorn* by the Royal Navy, they will commission with the Canadian Maritime Command as *Chicoutimi*, *Victoria*, *Cornerbrook* and *Windsor* respectively. Even allowing for the cost of refitting, these boats represent a considerable bargain having seen very little service prior to their transfer.

In Canadian service they will replace the three British-built Oberon class boats, some of which have already been laid up, and which are all well over 30 years old. To reduce costs, equipment from the Oberons, including American Mk.48 torpedoes, 18 of which can be stowed, and their associated fire control system, is being transferred to the new boats. In Royal Navy service the Upholders were equipped to fire the Harpoon SSM, but this facility has been removed prior to the transfer of ownership.

The Upholders are reputedly very quiet in operation and can dive to 650ft (200m). As with other modern diesel electric submarines, AIP is being considered for possible installation in the future.

SPECIFICATION

Type: SSK
Class: Victoria (Upholder, Type 2400)
Displacement: 2,168 tons surface, 2,455 tons dived
Length: 230.6ft (70.3m)
Beam: 25ft (7.6m)
Draught: 17.7ft (5.5m)
Machinery: diesel electric; 2 Paxman Valenta 16SZ diesels, 3,620hp; 2 GEC alternators, 2.8MW; 1 GEC motor, 5,400 hp; 1 shaft
Speed & Range: 12kt surface, 17kt dived; 9,000 miles (14,480km) at 12kt (surface)
Complement: 49
Missiles: nil
Guns: nil
ASW & USW: 6 21in (533mm) torpedo tubes, Mk.48 dual-purpose wire-guided torpedoes
Sensors: radar: Kelvin Hughes Type 1007 navigation; sonar: Thompson Sintra Type 2040 hull-mounted passive search and intercept; BAE Systems Type 2007 low-frequency passive array; Hermes/MUSL Type 2046 towed array
Aircraft: nil

SSK, Dolphin (Type 800)

THE ISRAELI NAVY MAINTAINS A small force of submarines and since 1977 this has comprised three small 420-ton Vickers Type 540 boats built in the UK and delivered in 1977. Despite their small size, they were armed with eight 21in (533mm) torpedo tubes and were modified to fire Sub Harpoon missiles.

The project to design and build their successors dates back to the 1980s, and in 1988 a contract was signed for two submarines to be built in Germany, although the US yard Ingalls Shipbuilding was designated as the prime contractor. However, this was cancelled for financial reasons, but a new order was placed in 1991 following the Gulf War and an option for a third boat was exercised in 1994. These were built in Germany by Howaldtswerke and Thyssen Nordseewerke, and the lead boat (*Dolphin*) was laid down in October 1994, launched on 12 April 1996 and commissioned in April 1999. A second boat, *Leviathan*, was completed the following month, and the third, *Tekuma*, was commissioned in mid 2000. The older Vickers boats were then withdrawn from service and may be sold to Ecuador.

The new Dolphin class represents a tremendous advance, being almost four times larger in terms of displacement and incorporating modern sonars and fire control equipment. Included in the package were stocks of STN Atlas DM2A3 wire-guided active homing torpedoes with a range of seven miles (11km). UGM-84C Sub Harpoon anti-ship missiles are also carried, and a total of 16 missiles and torpedoes can be stowed. The 26.6in (650mm) torpedo tubes are probably intended for swimmer delivery vehicles (SDV) to allow the conduct of clandestine operations. Israeli Navy submarines are painted blue and green to make them less visible in the special conditions of the eastern Mediterranean.

*Dolphin, **one of three ultra-modern SSKs now in service with the Israeli Navy.** (**Michael Nitz via Mönch Archives**)*

SPECIFICATION

Type: SSK
Class: Dolphin (Type 800)
Displacement: 1,640 tons surface, 1,900 tons dived
Length: 188ft (57.3m)
Beam: 22.3ft (6.8m)
Draught: 20.3ft (6.2m)
Machinery: 3 MTU 16V 396 SE84 diesels, 4,243hp; 3 alternators, 1 motor, 3,875hp; 1 shaft
Speed & Range: 20kt dived; 8,000 miles (12,870km) at 8kt (surface)
Complement: 30
Missiles: Boeing UGM-84C Sub Harpoon long-range SSM
Guns: nil
ASW & USW: 4 25.6in (650mm) tubes and 6 21in (533mm) torpedo tubes, DM2A3 wire-guided torpedoes; mines may be carried instead of torpedoes
Sensors: radar: Elta I-band surface search; sonar: Atlas CSU 90 hull-mounted active/passive search and attack
Aircraft: nil

SSK, Sauro/Improved Sauro

THE ORIGINAL SAURO CLASS was laid down from 1974 onwards, and the four boats of the class (*Nazario Sauro, Fecia dio Cossato, Leonardo da Vinci, Guglielmo Marconi*) were commissioned between 1980 and 1982. All four underwent a major modernisation refit in 1991–93 in which new, greater capacity batteries were fitted, auxiliary machinery was replaced and crew accommodation and habitability was much improved.

The main armament comprises 12 Whitehead A184 Mod. 3 wire-guided dual-purpose torpedoes with a maximum range of 15.5 miles (25km). Although all four boats remain in service, *Nazario Sauro* is used as a trials boat and is not maintained at operational readiness.

In 1983 two more boats of an Improved Sauro type were ordered, with a second pair ordered in July 1988. The first pair, *Salvatore Pelosi* and *Giuliano Prini*, were laid down in 1984 and 1985, and commissioned in 1988 and 1989. The other two, *Primo Longobardo* and *Gianfranco Gazzana Priaroggia*, followed in 1991/92 and were completed in 1994/95. These later boats had a very slightly lengthened hull (by a foot and a half, or half a metre) to allow for an additional watertight bulkhead and were constructed of stronger HY80 steel, permitting a normal maximum diving depth of 1,000ft (300m), some 165ft (50m) greater than the original Sauros. Armament still comprised the Whitehead torpedoes but there is provision for SSMs such as Harpoon to be fitted, although this option has not yet been exercised. All four Improved Sauros will be fitted with the STN Atlas ISUS 9020 integrated sonar system and an upgraded SACTIS fire control system during the course of modernisation refits between 1999 and 2002.

Primo Longobardo *(S524), one of four Improved Sauro class SSKs.* **(Marina Militare, Italy)**

Salvatore Pelosi *(S522). (D. Hannaford)*

Primo Longobardo *(S524).*
(Marina Militare, Italy)

SPECIFICATION

Type: SSK
Class: Sauro/Improved Sauro
Displacement: 1,476 tons surface, 1,662 tons dived
Length: 211.2ft (64.4m)
Beam: 22.3ft (6.8m)
Draught: 18.4ft (5.6m)
Machinery: diesel electric; 3 Fincantieri GMT210 16SM diesels; 3 generators, 2.16MW; 1 motor, 3,128hp; 1 shaft
Speed & Range: 11kt surface, 19kt dived; 12,650 miles (20,350km) at 11kt (surface)
Complement: 50
Missiles: Harpoon or Exocet may be carried at a future date
Guns: nil
ASW & USW: 6 21in (533mm) torpedo tubes, A184 dual-purpose wire-guided torpedoes
Sensors: radar: SMA BPS704 navigation and surface search; sonar: Selenia Elsag IPD70/S active/passive search and attack; MD100S passive ranging
Aircraft: nil

SSK, Type 212

Following the signing of a formal contract in 1994, construction of the lead boat began in July 1998 for completion in 2003, with another three due to commission in 2005/6. At around 1,450 tons, the Type 212 is considerably larger than its predecessors and this will extend its endurance and area of operations. The AIP system takes the form of PEM fuel cells which use hydrogen and oxygen to generate electricity, and this has resulted in an unusual pressure hull design. The forward section is a slightly flattened double hull while the after section, which houses all the propulsion system, has a smaller cross-section to allow the storage of the hydrogen and oxygen in cylinders external to the pressure hull (but within the hull casing). The fuel cells are integrated with diesel generators and conventional batteries, allowing considerable extra endurance on the new-design very efficient electric motors. Despite the increased size and sophistication of the Type 212, it requires a crew of only 27 who will benefit from much improved accommodation and a considerable degree of automation in routine tasks.

The Type 212 has also been selected by the Italian Navy, and two boats have been ordered which will be built by Fincantieri. These will be laid down in 2001/2 for completion in 2005/6.

The advanced Type 212 SSK is currently under construction for the German and Italian navies. (HDW/Thyssen)

THE GERMAN NAVY HAS ALWAYS BEEN one of the foremost proponents of submarine warfare and its current underwater fleet can trace its history back to the early 1960s when the Class 205 coastal submarines were laid down. These were followed by the slightly larger 450-ton Type 206 boats which were built between 1969 and 1975 and which proved to be very effective in the ASW role for which they were designed. Although larger and more modern designs have been built for other navies (e.g. Type 209, exported to 13 countries), there have been no new submarines for the German Navy for over 25 years. This situation is about to change with the introduction of the Type 212, an advanced design taking advantage of developments in air independent propulsion (AIP) systems.

SPECIFICATION

Type: SSK
Class: Type 212
Displacement: 1,450 tons surface, 1,830 tons dived
Length: 183.4ft (55.9m)
Beam: 23ft (7m)
Draught: 19.7ft (6m)
Machinery: 1 MTU 16V 396 diesel, 4,243hp; 1 alternator, 1 Siemens Permasyn motor, 3,875hp; 1 shaft; Siemens/HDW PEM AIP fuel cell system; high-energy batteries
Speed & Range: 20kt dived; 8,000 miles (12,870km) at 8kt (surface)
Complement: 27
Missiles: nil
Guns: nil
ASW & USW: 6 21in (533mm) torpedo tubes, DM 2A4 torpedoes; up to 16 mines in lieu of torpedoes; external containers carrying a total of 24 mines may also be fitted
Sensors: radar: Type 1007 navigation; sonar: DBQS-40 passive ranging and intercept; FAS-3 and TAS-3 flank and towed passive arrays; MOA 3070 or ELAK high-frequency active mine detection
Aircraft: nil

SSK, Gotland (A19)

DESPITE THEIR SMALL SIZE and conventional lines, these three submarines incorporate a major technical advance. Their propulsion system was designed from the start to include air independent propulsion (AIP) in the form of two Kockums-designed Stirling cycle engines in addition to standard diesel engines. AIP enables the submarine to operate underwater for several weeks without the use of a tell-tale snort mast.

The design was based on the previous Västergötland (A17) class of four 1,070-ton conventional diesel electric submarines built in Sweden between 1983 and 1990. The hull was lengthened to allow installation of two Kockums V4-275R Stirling Mk.2 engines, making the Gotland (A19) class the first in the world to be designed from the start to take advantage of this new technology, although a number of other countries are now following suit. Other improvements included a new sonar suite and upgraded weapons control system.

In addition to the lead boat, which commissioned in September 1996, a further two boats, *Uppland* and *Halland*, were completed in 1997. The Mk.2 Stirling motor uses a mixture of diesel fuel and liquid oxygen in a circular combustion unit. It is reported that this allows up to 19 days' endurance at slow speeds. An enhanced Mk.3 version will be retrofitted to two of the A17 class, *Södermanland* and *Östergötland*, in modernisation refits to be completed by 2003.

A sweeping reorganisation of the Swedish armed forces announced in November 1999 included a reduction of the submarine fleet from 10 to 5 boats, and these will be the three A19 class and the two modernised A17 class. Both classes can carry 12 torpedoes and up to 48 mines carried externally. The torpedoes may be replaced by the sophisticated Mk.47 swimming mine which is launched through the torpedo tubes and can then proceed to a predetermined position using its own propulsion system.

The Swedish Navy (Svenska Marinen), deploys three A19 Gotland class submarines. (CelsiusTech)

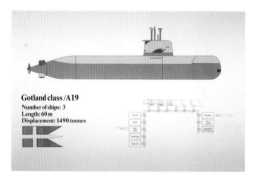

Gotland class /A19
Number of ships: 3
Length: 60 m
Displacement: 1490 tonnes

Drawing of a Gotland class SSK. (CelsiusTech)

SPECIFICATION

Type: SSK
Class: Gotland (A19)
Displacement: 1,240 tons surface, 1,490 tons dived
Length: 198.2ft (60.4m)
Beam: 20.3ft (6.2m)
Draught: 18.4ft (5.6m)
Machinery: diesel/AIP electric; 2 MTU diesels; 2 V4-275R Stirling AIP, 204hp; 1 Jeumont Schneider motor; 1 shaft
Speed & Range: 20kt dived
Complement: 25
Missiles: nil
Guns: nil
ASW & USW: 4 21in (533mm) torpedo tubes, FFV Type 613/62 or Bofors Type 62 wire-guided torpedoes; 2 15.75in (400mm) torpedo tubes, Type 432/451 wire-guided A/S torpedoes; Type 47 mines may be carried instead of torpedoes
Sensors: radar: I-band navigation; sonar: STN/Atlas CSU 90-2 passive search and attack with bow and flank arrays
Aircraft: nil

MAJOR WARSHIPS

FEW NAVIES CAN AFFORD TO BUILD and run large surface warships and consequently there are relatively few ships of this type in service today. The most significant are the massive Kirov class nuclear-powered cruisers of the Russian Navy which carry a staggering amount of weaponry in an armoured hull. Russia also has the Slava class cruisers, and these vessels are, to some extent, a substitute for the strike capability a carrier force would give. The US Navy has now decommissioned all its nuclear-powered cruisers of the California and Virginia classes, but has 27 conventionally powered Ticonderoga class Aegis cruisers optimised for the air defence role, although carrying a substantial offensive capability with cruise missiles. A number of navies still operate helicopter-carrying cruisers, a type of warship popular in the 1960s and 1970s among navies which could not aspire to fixed-wing carriers. Typical of these is the Italian *Vittorio Veneto*, and the French Navy still retains the *Jeanne d'Arc*, although this ship is used mainly for training purposes.

CGN, Kirov (Type 1144)

THESE ARE THE LARGEST surface combat ships, apart from aircraft carriers, to be laid down and completed by any nation since World War II, and for lack of any other suitable term are described as battlecruisers. They were also the first Russian surface warships to use a nuclear powerplant, although this is supplemented by a unique oil-fired system which boosts steam output by superheating.

The design originated in the late 1960s with the first of five projected ships laid down in 1973 and completed in 1980. This was the *Kirov*, later renamed *Admiral Ushakov*, and a second ship, *Admiral Lazarev*, was completed in 1984. Both of these have been decommissioned for some time and are now being scrapped. Two further ships, *Admiral Nakhimov* and *Pyotr Velikiy*, were completed in 1988 and 1998 respectively and remain in service. A fifth ship was scrapped while under construction in 1989.

The main armament of these imposing-looking ships is the battery of SS-N-19 Shipwreck surface-to-surface missiles contained in a launch silo on the long foredeck in which the missiles are angled at 45°. These are based on the earlier SS-N-12 but have a lower sea-skimming flight profile, although range and warheads are the same (300 miles, or 480km, and nuclear or HE). For self-defence, the Kirovs bristle with various surface-to-air missile systems and gun-based CIWS. Reportedly over 500 such missiles are carried. A powerful anti-submarine armament is also carried, including three Kamov Ka-27 Helix anti-submarine helicopters which operate from a stern flightdeck served by lifts from the hangar below. The helicopters are also tasked with providing over-the-horizon targeting data for the SS-N-19 missiles.

With their powerful offensive and defensive weapons systems, and the nuclear propulsion, the Kirovs are capable of sustained independent

Above and below left: *Kirov (Type 1144) nuclear-powered battlecruiser. (RAF Kinloss/MoD)*

operations, but they were also intended to provide powerful support for the large aircraft carriers which were planned. With only one of these now in service, the role of the two remaining cruisers is limited and they are expensive to run as well as requiring large crews.

SPECIFICATION

Type: CGN

Class: Kirov (Type 1144)

Displacement: 19,000 tons standard, 24,300 tons full load

Length: 826.8ft (252m)

Beam: 93.5ft (28.5m)

Draught: 29.5ft (9.1m)

Machinery: CONAS; 2 KN-3 PWR reactors, 300MW; 2 boilers; 2 GT3A-688 turbines, 140,000hp; 2 shafts

Speed & Range: 30kt; 14,000 miles (22,500km) at 30kt

Complement: 744

Missiles: 20 tube VLS silo, SS-N-19 Shipwreck long-range SSM; 12 vertical launchers, SA-N-6 Grumble long-range SAM; 2 twin launchers, SA-N-4 Gecko short-range SAM; 2 octuple vertical launchers, SA-N-9 Gauntlet short-range SAM; 6 octuple launchers co-located on 30mm gun mounts (see below), SA-N-11 Grisson short-range SAM

Guns: 2 twin 130mm (5.1in)/70 AK130 automatic guns; 6 twin multi-barrelled 30mm CADS-N-1 CIWS (includes launchers for SA-N-11 missiles)

ASW & USW: 2 quintuple torpedo tubes, various 12in (305mm) torpedoes; fixed tubes in superstructure can launch Type 40 torpedoes or SS-N-15 torpedo-carrying A/S missiles; 1 10-barrelled RBU 12000 A/S mortar; 2 6-barrelled RBU 1000 A/S mortars

Sensors: radar: Top Pair long-range 3D air search; Top Plate 3D air and surface search; Palm Frond navigation; Cross Sword, Top Dome, Flap Lid/Tomb Stone, Pop Group, Kite Screech and Hot Flash fire control; Flyscreen aircraft control; sonar: Horse Jaw, hull-mounted active search and attack; Horse Tail active VDS search and attack

Aircraft: 3 helicopters

CVH, Jeanne d'Arc

Jeanne d'Arc (R97), helicopter carrier and training cruiser.
(Marine Nationale)

ONE OF THE MOST VENERABLE major warships afloat today, the *Jeanne d'Arc* was laid down at Brest Naval Dockyard on 7 July 1960, launched on 30 September 1961 and commissioned on 16 July 1964. She was originally designed as a multi-role helicopter cruiser and was to have been armed with the Masurca medium-range surface-to-air missile. When completed, the Masurca was deleted, but in 1975 her offensive capabilities were enhanced by the addition of six Exocet anti-ship missiles to back up the four single 3.9in (100mm) guns. Her main role has been as a training ship for French Navy cadets, and she replaced a training cruiser of the same name which had been launched in 1930. In fact, she originally bore the name *La Résolue* when first commissioned, retaining that name until the older ship was decommissioned in 1965.

Each year, in the autumn and spring, she usually makes extensive training cruises, and has completed well over 30 over the years, helping to train whole generations of naval officers. While engaged in this role she usually carries a number of ASW helicopters and can provide support to other task groups. In wartime she would embark up to eight helicopters (a mixture of Super Pumas and Lynxes) to assume her major role as an ASW helicopter cruiser. However, she can also deploy in the commando carrier role, able to accommodate a battalion of up to 700 marines or troops.

Altogether she has proved to be an extremely flexible and useful vessel, and has already given 36 years of service. Following a major refit in 1997/98, it is expected that the *Jeanne d'Arc* will remain in service until 2005.

SPECIFICATION

Type: CVH
Class: Jeanne d'Arc
Displacement: 10,000 tons standard, 13,270 tons full load
Length: 597.1ft (182m)
Beam: 78.7ft (24m)
Draught: 24ft (7.3m)
Machinery: 4 boilers, 2 Tateau-Bretange turbines, 40,000hp; 2 shafts
Speed & Range: 27kt; 6,000 miles (9,650km) at 15kt
Complement: 626
Missiles: 2 fixed triple launchers, Exocet MM38 medium-range SSM
Guns: 4 DCN 3.9in (100mm)/55 CADAM automatic; 4 12.7mm (0.5in) machine-guns
ASW & USW: nil
Sensors: radar: DRBV 22D long-range air search; DRBV 50 surface search; DRBN 34A navigation; DRBC 32A fire control
Aircraft: up to 8 helicopters

CG, Slava (Type 1164)

Above and right: Marshal Ustinov, *one of three Slava class (Type 1164) missile-armed cruisers.* **(RAF Kinloss/MoD)**

POWERFULLY ARMED MISSILE CRUISERS, the Slava class ships are effectively smaller versions of the Kirovs with a conventional propulsion system, although the combination of no fewer than six gas turbines is unique in naval construction. The most prominent identification feature is the serried rows of fixed launchers for the SS-N-12 Sandbox surface-to-surface missiles either side of the forward superstructure. These have a range of around 300 miles (480km) at a speed of Mach 1.7 and can carry either a 350-kiloton nuclear warhead or a conventional 2,200lb (1,000kg) HE warhead. Less easily spotted are the vertical launch silos for the SA-N-6 Grumble area defence surface-to-air missiles, which are installed in the deck immediately abaft the twin funnels. A total of 64 of these missiles are carried and they are capable of engaging aerial targets up to an altitude of 90,000ft (27,450m) and at ranges in excess of 50 miles (80km). At the stern is a flightdeck and hangar for the single Kamov Ka-27 helicopter whose main function is to provide over-the-horizon targeting information for the SS-N-12 missiles. Alternatively, such information can be derived via the Punch Bowl SATCOM system.

Three ships (*Moskva*, *Marshal Ustinov*, *Varyag*) were laid down in the 1970s and these were completed between 1982 and 1989. A fourth ship, the *Admiral Lobov*, was laid down in 1984 and, following the break-up of the Soviet Union, was allocated to the Ukraine Navy. However, it was transferred back to Russia in 1995 but has yet to be completed, and may even be re-allocated to the Ukraine. Plans for a fifth ship appear to have been abandoned in 1990. *Marshal Ustinov* is allocated to the Northern fleet while *Varyag* has been with the Pacific fleet since 1990. *Moskva* will become the Black Sea fleet flagship on completion of its refit in 2000.

SPECIFICATION

Type: CG
Class: Slava (Type 1164)
Displacement: 9,800 tons standard, 11,200 tons full load
Length: 610.2ft (186m)
Beam: 70.5ft (21.5m)
Draught: 24.9ft (7.6m)
Machinery: COGAG; 4 gas turbines, 88,000hp; 2 gas turbines, 20,000hp; 2 shafts
Speed & Range: 32kt; 7,500 miles (12,060km) at 15kt
Complement: 454
Missiles: 8 fixed twin launchers, SS-N-12 long-range SSM; 8 vertical launch tubes, SA-N-6 Grumble long-range SAM; 2 twin launchers, SA-N-4 Gecko short-range SAM
Guns: 1 twin 130mm (5.1in)/70 automatic; 6 AK130 6-barrelled 30mm CIWS
ASW & USW: 2 quintuple 21in (533mm) torpedo tubes, various torpedoes; 2 RBU 6000 12-barrelled A/S mortars
Sensors: radar: Top Pair long-range 3D air search; Top Steer or Top Plate 3D air and surface search; Palm Frond navigation; Front Door, Top Dome, Pop Group, Bass Tilt and Kite Screech fire control; sonar: Bull Horn and Steer Hide hull-mounted low-/medium-frequency active search and attack
Aircraft: 1 helicopter

UNITED STATES
CG, Ticonderoga

A TOTAL OF 27 TICONDEROGA CLASS AEGIS cruisers were commissioned between 1983 and 1994, allocated hull nos. CG-47 to CG-73. Developed at the height of the Cold War, these ships were equipped with the Aegis air defence system comprising a phased array radar with provision for multiple simultaneous engagement of aircraft and anti-ship missile targets using Standard surface-to-air missiles in order to defeat a potential attack from a massed formation of Russian Badger or Backfire maritime strike aircraft. The first five ships (CG-47 to CG-51) were armed with two twin Mk.26 missile launchers capable of firing Standard SAMs or ASROC A/S missiles. However, the remaining ships were fitted with two Mk.41 vertical launch silos which, as well as firing the Standard missile, could also accommodate Tomahawk cruise missiles.

In outline these ships closely resemble the slightly smaller Spruance class destroyers on which the design is based (in fact, the name ship was originally designated DDG-47). The obvious external difference is the slab-sided phased array antennae of the SPY-1 radar around the bridge and on the after superstructure.

In a construction programme lasting well over a decade there have been continuous developments of weapons systems and electronic equipment so that there have been several subvariants of the basic design, referred to as Baseline 0 to Baseline VII. Progressive improvements introduced include LAMPS III helicopters, improved versions of the Standard SM-2 missile, SQQ-89 sonar, advanced SPY-1B radar and displays, upgraded computer systems, JTIDS Link-16, Tomahawk SLCM and associated fire control equipment, and a theatre ballistic missile defence system (TBMD). Two ships, *Lake Erie* (CG-70) and *Vella Gulf* (CG-72), have been modified to incorporate TBMD and are currently carrying out trials of this, the first naval defence against ballistic missiles.

One of the earlier vessels, *Yorktown* (CG-48), was modified in 1996 as the US Navy's first Smart Ship. This project utilised modern advanced technology to automate many tasks associated with navigation, machinery control and damage control in order to reduce the complement by 46. Following successful trials, this concept will be applied to other ships of the class.

USS Gettysburg (CG-64) Ticonderoga class Aegis cruiser.
(US Navy)

SPECIFICATION

Type: CG
Class: Ticonderoga
Displacement: 7,015 tons standard, up to 9,516 tons full load
Length: 567ft (172.8m)
Beam: 55ft (16.8m)
Draught: 31ft (9.5m)
Machinery: 4 GE LM2500 gas turbines, 86,000hp; 2 shafts, cp propellers
Speed & Range: 30kt +; 6,000 miles (9,650km) at 20kt
Complement: 405 (max.)
Missiles: Mk.41 VLS Tomahawk SLCM (not first 5 ships), Mk.41 VLS or 2 Mk.26 twin launchers, Standard SM-2MR medium-range SAM; 2 quadruple launchers, Boeing Harpoon SSM and SLAM
Guns: 2 single 5in (127mm)/45 Mk.45 automatic guns; 2 Vulcan/Phalanx 20mm CIWS
ASW & USW: 2 Mk.26 twin launchers, ASROC (first 5 ships only); 2 triple 324mm (12.75in) torpedo tubes, Mk.46 A/S torpedoes
Sensors: radar: SPY-1A or 1B phased array 3D combined air search and fire control (Aegis); SPS-49(V)7 or 8 long-range air search; SPS-55 surface search; SPS-64(V)9 navigation; SPQ-9A and SPG-62 fire control; sonar: SQS-53B bow-mounted medium-frequency active search and attack or SQQ-89(V)3 combined hull-mounted active and towed passive array; SQR-19 TACTASS passive towed array (2 ships only)
Aircraft: 2 helicopters

USS Vicksburg (CG-69), Ticonderoga class Aegis cruiser. (Maritime Photographic)

CGH, Vittorio Veneto

THE *VITTORIO VENETO* WAS ORIGINALLY projected as far back as 1959 but construction did not commence until 1965 and she was commissioned on 12 July 1969. The design was similar to two ships of the Andrea Doria class laid down in 1958, but was considerably larger to allow the operation of more helicopters and to carry a substantially more powerful armament. An interesting innovation was the dual-purpose missile launcher which could handle both Terrier SAMs and ASROC ASW missiles. This saved weight and space, and the idea was subsequently adopted by the US Navy. The Terrier missiles were later replaced by the current Standard SM-1ER SAMs, and a modernisation refit from 1981 to 1984 resulted in the addition of the twin 40mm with the Dardo/SPG-74 fire control system for defence against sea-skimming missiles, as well as the Teseo long-range anti-ship missiles.

Unusually for a modern warship, the *Vittorio Veneto* carries a substantial gun armament with no fewer than eight single 76mm (3in) guns scattered around the superstructure and the three twin 40mm disposed one forward and two aft on either side of the flightdeck. Prominent above the forward superstructure are the antennae of the two SPG-55C tracking radars for the Standard missiles, while the funnel uptakes are hidden in two substantial 'macks' carrying the SPS-52C and SPS-702 search radars as well as other electronic equipment. The flightdeck and hangar facilities support up to six Agusta Bell AB 212 helicopters equipped with search radar and AQS-13B dipping sonar for ASW tasks. However, a dual-purpose ship such as this is always a compromise and a true carrier such as the *Garibaldi* offers much greater flexibility.

The *Vittorio Veneto* is due to remain in service until at least 2007 when she will be replaced by the *Luigi Einaudi*, a 22,000-ton carrier intended mainly for amphibious warfare but capable of operating fixed-wing Harriers as well as Merlin helicopters.

The helicopter cruiser **Vittorio Veneto** *(C550) will remain in service until 2007. (Marina Militare, Italy)*

The helicopter cruiser **Vittorio Veneto** *(C550). (Marina Militare, Italy)*

SPECIFICATION

Type: CGH
Class: Vittorio Veneto
Displacement: 7,500 tons standard, 9,500 tons full load
Length: 589ft (179.6m)
Beam: 63.6ft (19.4m)
Draught: 19.7ft (6m)
Machinery: steam turbine; 4 Foster Wheeler boilers, 2 turbines, 73,000hp; 2 shafts
Speed & Range: 32kt; 5,000 miles (8,050km) at 17kt
Complement: 557
Missiles: 4 single fixed launchers, OTO Melera Teseo long-range SSM; 1 Aster Mk.10 twin launcher, Standard SM-1ER medium-range SAM
Guns: 8 OTO Melera 3in (76mm)/62 MMK automatic guns; 3 Breda twin 40mm
ASW & USW: 2 Mk.32 triple 324mm (12.75in) torpedo tubes, Mk.46 A/S torpedoes; SLQ-25 Nixie torpedo decoy
Sensors: radar: SPS-52C long-range 3D air search; SPS-768 air search; SPS-702 surface search/target indication; SPS-748 navigation; SPG-70, SPG-74, SPG-55C fire control; sonar: SQS-23G bow-mounted medium-frequency active search and attack
Aircraft: 6 helicopters

DESTROYERS & FRIGATES

THE BACKBONE of any modern navy is its fleet of destroyers and frigates, although the distinction between the two types has become increasingly blurred as most of the latest ships are capable of a wide variety of operational roles. In modern terminology a frigate is generally regarded as having a predominantly ASW role while a destroyer is normally optimised for the AAW role, deploying a medium- or long-range surface-to-air weapons system for area defence, and is also normally a larger ship. However, these distinctions have become increasingly blurred as many modern warships combine the two roles, and some navies have a habit of designating their larger ships as destroyers even though they carry only a short-range point defence missile system. The French Georges Leygues class is a case in point. Conversely, some very large, well-armed ships are still designated as frigates. For that reason the two types are described here in a single section. In the case of smaller navies, their destroyers and frigates are their major assets and consequently are designed to undertake a wide variety of roles.

UNITED STATES
DDG, Arleigh Burke

NUMERICALLY THE ARLEIGH BURKE (DDG-51) class Aegis destroyers are the most significant element of the US Navy surface fleet. In all, 28 ships were commissioned between 1991 and 1999, these being designated Flight I and Flight II, the latter featuring improved electronic systems and greater fuel capacity which resulted in an increase in full load displacement.

Flight I ships were armed with the Standard SM-2MR Block 4 missile which could engage targets up to 45 miles (73km) away but the Flight II introduced the SM-2ER with a range of 83 miles (134km). In addition, all versions can carry up to 56 Tomahawk TLAM-C/D cruise missiles with a range of 810 miles (1,300 km). Both Flight I and II ships have a flightdeck on the stern equipped with basic facilities for refuelling and re-arming SH-60 Seahawk helicopters, but lack of a hangar meant that a helicopter could not be permanently embarked. This questionable deficiency was addressed in the revised Flight IIA ships, starting with DDG-79, Oscar Austin, launched in 1998, which features a lengthened stern to expand the flightdeck and twin hangars set into the after-section of the weather deck. As a result these ships can now embark two SH-60B or F Seahawk helicopters which can be employed in the anti-ship role carrying Penguin air-to-surface missiles, as well as perform normal ASW duties. Flight IIA ships also have an enhanced missile armament with a 32-cell Mk.41 VLS forward and a 64-cell VLS aft (compared to 29/61 cells in earlier ships).

Currently some 20 Flight IIA ships are on order with the first three commissioning in 2000 and the remainder by 2005. Further orders are likely.

All DDG-51 class ships carry a single Mk.45 automatic 5in (127mm)/54 calibre gun firing 20 rounds per minute over ranges up to 14 miles (23km). However, a modified 62-calibre barrel can be fitted which would enable the gun to fire ERGM rounds, which are fitted with GPS to enable them to hit targets with an accuracy of 32ft (10m) at ranges of almost 93 miles (150km). They are also fitted with the Kingfisher hull-mounted mine detection system, and may also receive a remote minehunting system in the future as a result of experiences in the 1991 Gulf War

USS **Benfold** *(DDG-65) and USS* **Stethem** *(DDG-63). (Ingalls Shipbuilding)*

when several valuable ships were severely damaged by mines.

The successor to the DDG-51 will be the new DD-21, a 32-ship programme to replace current Spruance class destroyers and Perry class frigates. Sometimes referred to as the Land Attack Destroyer, the DD-21 will be a revolutionary design having a 256-cell VLS capable of firing a full array of missiles, possibly including a land attack version of the Standard SAM, a very sophisticated command, control and communication computer system, new gun systems, possibly a new propulsion system, and all this encased in an advanced stealth hull with few projections or protuberances. The lead ship should be laid down in 2005 for completion in 2010.

SPECIFICATION

Type: DDG
Class: Arleigh Burke
Displacement: 8,422 tons standard, up to 9,217 tons full load
Length: 504.5ft (153.8m)
Beam: 66.9ft (20.4m)
Draught: hull 20.7ft (6.3m)
Machinery: 4 GE LM2500 gas turbines, 105,000hp; 2 shafts, cp propellers
Speed & Range: 32kt; 4,400 miles (7,080km) at 20kt
Complement: 346
Missiles: 2 quadruple fixed launchers, Boeing Harpoon long-range SSM; 2 Mk.41 VLS, Tomahawk SLCM and Standard SM-2MR SAM
Guns: 1 5in (127mm)/54 Mk.45 automatic gun; 2 Vulcan/Phalanx 6-barrelled 20mm CIWS
ASW & USW: ASROC VLA (fired from Mk.41 launchers); 2 Mk.32 triple 324mm (12.75in) torpedo tubes; Mk.46 A/S torpedoes
Sensors: radar: SPY-1D phased array air search and fire control (Aegis); SPS-67 surface search; SPS-64 navigation; SPG-62 fire control; sonar: SQQ-89 comprising SQS-53C bow-mounted active search and attack; and SQR-19B TACTAS passive towed array
Aircraft: 2 helicopters
(Note: data applies to Flight I ships – see text)

USS **Milius** *(DDG-69), Arleigh Burke class (Flight I). (Ingalls Shipbuilding)*

DDG, Kongo

Above and left: Myoukou (DDG-175), Kongo class Aegis-equipped destroyer of the JMSDF. (Guy Toremans)

In view of the proximity of Japan to parts of China, Korea and Russia, the Kongo class ships can provide a useful addition to the air defence of the mainland, in addition to their purely naval tasks. In this the JMSDF is not unique, as the British Type 42 destroyers have a similar role in the North Sea.

BASED ON THE US ARLEIGH BURKE CLASS, these ships are slightly larger and are equipped with an export version of the Aegis air defence system, integrating the Standard SM-2MR surface-to-air missiles with phased array, track while scan, SPY-1 radar. This version of the Standard missile has a range of 47 miles (75km) but may eventually be replaced by the improved SM-3. Japan was the first nation permitted to receive the Aegis system, although there were some reservations expressed in Congress over this action and the actual transfer of equipment and technology was somewhat delayed. Subsequently, however, Aegis equipment has also been exported to Spain.

All four ships of the Kongo class were built in Japan and were laid down between 1990 and 1995. Kongo was completed in 1993 and was followed by Kirishima (1995), Myoukou (1996) and Choukai (1998). Plans to build further ships were abandoned due to the high cost of the Aegis system. In appearance they are almost identical to the US Arleigh Burke class, the main difference being the use of a lattice foremast instead of the raked tripod on the American ships. Although the US ships now incorporate hangar facilities for a helicopter, the Kongo class ships retain the original landing platform arrangement with only limited facilities for helicopter operations.

SPECIFICATION

Type: DDG
Class: Kongo
Displacement: 7,250 tons standard, 9,485 tons full load
Length: 528.2ft (161m)
Beam: 68.9ft (21m)
Draught: hull 20.3ft (6.2m)
Machinery: COGAG; 4 LM2500 gas turbines, 102,160hp; 2 shafts, cp propellers
Speed & Range: 30kt; 4,500 miles (7,240km) at 20kt
Complement: 7
Missiles: 2 quadruple fixed launchers, Boeing Harpoon SSM; 2 Mk.41 VLS (28 and 61 cells), Standard SM-2MR SAM
Guns: 1 OTO Melera 5in (127mm)/54 automatic gun; 2 Vulcan/Phalanx 6-barrelled 20mm CIWS
ASW & USW: ASROC A/S missiles (launched from Mk.41 VLS); 2 triple 324mm (12.75in) torpedo tubes, Mk.46 A/S torpedo; SLQ-25 towed decoy
Sensors: radar: SPY-1D long-range 3D air search; OPS-28D surface search; OPS-20 navigation; SPG-62 fire control; sonar: SQS-53B/C bow-mounted search and attack; SQR-19A TACTASS passive towed array
Aircraft: helicopter platform but no helicopter permanently embarked

DDG, Delhi

Above: INS Delhi *(D61). First of a class of three destroyers being built in India. (Guy Toremans)*

Right: Stern view of Delhi *showing a Sea King helicopter on the flightdeck. (Guy Toremans)*

AS A PROFESSED NEUTRAL POWER, India has looked to all sources for arms supplies but has increasingly turned to Russia for the supply of warships and naval armaments. Their first large modern destroyers were the five Rajput class built for the Indian Navy at Nikolayev in the Ukraine between 1977 and 1987. These 4,000-ton vessels were based on the Russian Kashin II and are powered by four gas turbines giving a speed of 35kt. A powerful armament includes Styx anti-ship missiles and Goa medium-range surface-to-air missiles. A twin 3in (76mm) gun is carried as well as 30mm CIWS, while torpedoes and ASW mortars complete the armament outfit. Right aft is a flightdeck and hangar for a single Ka-27 or 28 Helix helicopter.

As a follow-on to the Rajput class, three large destroyers were ordered from Mazagon Dock Ltd at Bombay. These are the Delhi class, and the name ship was laid down in 1987 and launched in February 1991, although the subsequent completion was delayed by problems with Russian equipment suppliers, so she did not commission until November 1997. The second and third ships, *Mysore* and *Bombay*, were laid down in 1991 and 1992, and were completed in 1999 and 2000 respectively,

The design loosely follows that of the Rajputs in outline but there are considerable differences in equipment and armament and the ships present a less cluttered outline. A CODOG machinery system is adopted and a conventional two-funnel arrangement replaces the bulky four uptake system on the earlier ships. This frees up deck space allowing a conventional hangar and flightdeck aft, large enough to accommodate two Sea King Mk.42 ASW helicopters. A 50ft (15m) lengthening of the hull allows full load displacement to rise by 1,700 tons, and a very powerful and balanced armament is fitted. However, continuing problems with Russian suppliers may result in more western equipment being fitted in the future.

SPECIFICATION

Type: DDG
Class: Delhi
Displacement: 6,700 tons full load
Length: 534.8ft (163m)
Beam: 55.8ft (17m)
Draught: 21.3ft (6.5m)
Machinery: CODOG; 2 AM-50 Ukraine gas turbines, 54,000hp; 2 KVM-18 diesels, 9,920hp; 2 shafts, cp propellers
Speed & Range: 28kt
Complement: 360
Missiles: 4 quadruple fixed launchers, SS-N-25 (KH-35 Uran) long-range SSM; 2 single launchers, SA-N-7 Gadfly medium-range SAM
Guns: 1 3.9in (100mm)/59 AK100 automatic gun; 4 AK630 6-barrelled 30mm CIWS
ASW & USW: 1 quintuple 21in (533mm) torpedo tubes, SET65E and Type 53-65 A/S torpedoes
Sensors: radar: Bharat Signaal LW08 long-range air search; Half Plate air and surface search; Bharat Rashmi and Palm Frond navigation; Front Dome, Kite Screech, Bass Tilt, Plank Shave fire control; sonar: APSOH hull-mounted medium-frequency search and attack; Model 15-750 VDS
Aircraft: 2 helicopters

FFG, Udaloy

OFFICIALLY CLASSIFIED AS TYPE 1155 large anti-submarine ships, these heavily armed vessels are larger than many destroyers. A total of 11 Udaloys were completed between 1981 and 1991 but only seven are currently available. An additional ship to a slightly modified design (Type 1155.1), the *Admiral Chabanenko*, commissioned in 1995 as the first of a projected Udaloy II class, but no others were laid down.

From a recognition point of view, the Udaloy class ships are easily distinguished by the unusual combination of four funnels in two pairs, and two separate hangars serving the flightdeck on the stern. These latter each house a single Ka-27 Helix-A ASW helicopter. Other ASW weapons include various types of 21in (533mm) homing torpedoes and the RBU 6000 trainable 12-barrelled A/S rocket launcher. Prominent on either side of the forward super-structure are the angled launchers for the SS-N-14 Silex missiles which can be configured as ASW missiles to deliver a Type 40 or Type E53-72 torpedo out to a range of 34 miles (55km). Alternatively they can carry a five-kiloton nuclear depth charge or be configured as an anti-ship missile carrying a 1,100lb (500kg) conventional warhead. For air defence the ship is armed with SA-N-9 Gauntlet missiles fired from eight vertical launch containers, of which four are set into the foredeck and the others are located around the superstructure. Two single automatic 3.9in (100mm) guns are mounted forward, each firing 60 rounds per minute. The single Type 1155.1 differs mainly in that the guns are replaced by one twin 130mm (5.1in) mounting and the after-shelter deck plating is extended aft to enclose the trainable torpedo tubes.

Two more of these ships were projected but one was scrapped while being built and the other was never laid down.

Admiral Levchenko, *Udaloy Type 1155 ASW ship.* (RAF Kinloss/MoD)

Admiral Levchenko, *Udaloy Type 1155 ASW ship.* (RAF Kinloss/MoD)

SPECIFICATION

Type: FFG
Class: Udaloy
Displacement: 6,700 tons standard, 8,500 tons full load
Length: 534.6ft (163.5m)
Beam: 63.3ft (19.3m)
Draught: 24.6ft (7.5m)
Machinery: COGAG; 2 gas turbines 55,500hp; 2 cruising gas turbines, 13,600hp; 2 shafts
Speed & Range: 29kt; 7,700 miles (12,340km) at 18kt
Complement: 249
Missiles: 8 vertical launchers, SA-N-9 Gauntlet short-range SAM
Guns: 2 single 3.9in (100mm)/59 automatic guns; 4 AK630 6-barrelled 30mm CIWS
ASW & USW: 2 quadruple launchers, SS-N-14 Silex long-range anti-submarine missiles carrying a nuclear warhead or an A/S torpedo; 2 quadruple torpedo tubes, 21in (533mm) torpedoes; 2 RBU 6000 12-barrelled A/S mortars
Sensors: radar: Strut Pair air search; Top Plate 3D air search; Palm Frond surface search; Eye Bowl, Cross Sword, Kite Screech and Bass Tilt fire control; sonar: Horse Jaw hull-mounted low-/medium-frequency active search and attack; Mouse Tail medium-frequency active search VDS
Aircraft: 2 helicopters

DDG, Spruance

ORIGINALLY SOME 31 SPRUANCE CLASS destroyers were built between 1972 and 1983, but only 24 are currently active. Unusually for such a large destroyer, they were not designed to carry a medium- or long-range surface-to-air missile for area defence, the only anti-aircraft missiles being the short-range Sea Sparrow in an eight-cell trainable launcher on the stern. A flightdeck is incorporated into the after-section of the main superstructure with a large hangar immediately beside the second funnel, which is itself offset well to starboard. The fore funnel is similarly offset to port, and this reflects the layout of the machinery rooms which contain the four LM2500 gas turbines and two gas-turbine-driven generating sets. In fact, the Spruance class destroyers were the first major US warships to be entirely powered by gas turbines. Originally they were intended to be 'air capable' ships carrying four ASW helicopters, but the cost of this proved to be prohibitive and the ships were completed with facilities for a single SH-2 LAMPS I or SH-3 Sea King helicopter. Current ships operate the SH-60B or SH-2G LAMPS III helicopter.

On the foredeck was a multiple ASROC launcher, later flanked by armoured quadruple launchers for Tomahawk cruise missiles. From 1986 onwards a substantial modernisation programme began, the most notable change being the deletion of these separate missile launchers in favour of the versatile Mk.41 vertical launch system which could fire both ASROC and Tomahawk. There is also provision to launch Standard SM-2MR surface-to-air missiles, although these would then be controlled by other, Aegis-equipped, ships.

The basic Spruance hull and machinery has proved very adaptable and it formed the basis for the later Ticonderoga class cruisers. In addition, four Spruances were completed to a modified design as the Kidd class, completed 1981/82. These were dedicated AAW ships with twin launchers fore and aft for Standard MR-2MR surface-to-air missiles. Harpoon and ASROC could also be carried. However, the introduction of the Aegis-equipped Ticonderogas made these ships obsolete and they have been laid up for some time.

USS Briscoe (DD-977). (US Navy)

Both the Australian and Greek navies have expressed an interest in acquiring them, but nothing positive has transpired to date.

SPECIFICATION

Type: DDG
Class: Spruance
Displacement: 5,770 tons standard, 8,040 tons full load
Length: 563.2ft (171.7m)
Beam: 55.1ft (16.8m)
Draught: hull 19ft (5.8m)
Machinery: 4 GE LM2500 gas turbines, 86,000hp; 2 shafts, cp propellers
Speed & Range: 33kt; 6,000 miles (9,650km) at 20kt
Complement: 339 (max.)
Missiles: 2 quadruple launchers, Boeing Harpoon SSM; Mk.41 VLS silo for Tomahawk TLAM-C/D land attack cruise missile; Mk.29 octuple launcher, Sea Sparrow short-range SAM; 1 quadruple launcher, RAM short-range SAM
Guns: 2 single 5in (127mm)/54 Mk.45 automatic guns; 2 Vulcan/Phalanx 6-barrelled 20mm CIWS; 4 12.7mm (0.5in) machine-guns
ASW & USW: 2 enclosed Mk.32 triple 324mm (12.75in) torpedo tubes, Mk.46 A/S torpedoes; ASROC VLA (launched from Mk.41 VLS)
Sensors: radar: SPS-40 long-range air search; Hughes Mk.23 target designator; SPS-55 surface search; SPS-64(V)9 navigation; SPQ-9A and Raytheon Mk.95 fire control; sonar: SQQ-89 comprising SQS-53C bow-mounted active search and attack and SQR-19 TACTAS passive towed array
Aircraft: 2 helicopters

USS Inglestone (DD-990), a Spruance class destroyer currently laid up in reserve. (US Navy)

DDG, Sovremenny (Type 956/956A)

THESE ARE POWERFUL AND IMPOSING SHIPS with a typical Russian outfit of offensive weaponry intended primarily for the surface warfare role. Although the armament includes batteries of SSMs and SAMs, the Sovremenny class destroyers were notable for introducing a powerful new automatic 130mm (5.1in) gun carried in twin mountings fore and aft. With a rate of fire of up to 45 rounds per minute, these can lay down a tremendous weight of fire within a very short time.

One result of positioning a gun mounting right aft is that the helicopter flightdeck is positioned well forward where it is less susceptible to pitching movement. The single Kamov Ka-27 helicopter is housed in a folding hangar which retracts into the superstructure abaft the funnel, although the relative position of the latter may cause turbulence problems for the helicopter approaching to land.

Early Sovremennys were designated Type 956, but the last few were equipped to fire improved SS-N-22 missiles, with the range increased from 68 miles (110km) to 100 miles (160km), and SA-N-17 SAMs instead of the SS-N-7. These were designated Type 956A. Construction of the lead ship began in 1976 and a total of 17 Sovremennys were built for the Russian Navy, although only 8 currently remain available for operational tasks. Two more were sold to China while under construction and the first (*Hangzhou*) was launched in 1998 and sailed for China early in 2000. The second was launched at St Petersburg on 16 April 2000 and is due to be completed in 2002. Negotiations to purchase up to three more, known as Type 956E, will probably wait until the PLAN has fully evaluated its existing ships. The Chinese vessels are armed with SS-N-22 Sunburn SSMs, SA-N-7 Gadfly or SA-N-17 Grizzly SAMs, four 130mm (5.1in) guns, four AK-630 CIWS and ASW torpedoes, mortars and rockets.

SPECIFICATION

Type: DDG

Class: Sovremenny (Type 956/956A)

Displacement: 6,600 tons standard, 7,940 tons full load

Length: 511.8ft (156m)

Beam: 56.8ft (17.3m)

Draught: 21.3ft (6.5m)

Machinery: 4 boilers, 2 GTZA-674 turbines, 99,500hp; 2 shafts; bow thruster

Speed & Range: 32kt; 6,500 miles (10,460km) at 20kt

Complement: 296

Missiles: 2 fixed quadruple launchers, SS-N-22 Sunburn SSM; 2 single launchers, SA-N-7 Gadfly or SA-N-17 Grizzly medium-range SAM

Guns: 2 twin 130mm (5.1in) AK130 automatic guns; 4 AK630 6-barrelled 30mm CIWS

ASW & USW: 2 twin 21in (553mm) torpedo tubes, various A/S and anti-surface torpedoes available, including some with nuclear warheads; 2 6-barrelled RBU1000 A/S rocket launchers

Sensors: radar: Top Plate long-range 3D air search; Palm Frond surface search; Front Dome, Kite Screech, Bass Tilt fire control; sonar: Bull Horn and Whale Tongue hull-mounted medium-frequency active search and attack

Aircraft: 1 helicopter

DDG, Shirane/Haruna

THESE ARE LARGE HELICOPTER-CARRYING destroyers specialising in the anti-submarine role. The two ships of the Shirane class (Shirane and Kurama) were laid down in 1977/78 and completed in 1980/81. They were a development of the earlier Haruna class completed in 1973/74 and of a very similar design. The later ships were slightly larger, a 20ft (6m) longer hull allowing a 200-ton increase in standard displacement, and can be distinguished by their two separate funnels, as opposed to the split trunk single funnel of the Harunas, and these are offset, the fore funnel to port and the after one to starboard. A prominent feature is the large hangar amidships with a large flightdeck leading aft. This can accommodate three SH-60J helicopters, giving a substantial ASW capability to back up the ships' own Mk.46 torpedoes and ASROC missiles. The latter are fired from an eight-cell launcher on the foredeck immediately below the bridge. The two automatic Mk.42 5in (127mm)/54 calibre guns can each fire 24 rounds per minute (maximum) to a range of 15 miles (24km), providing very useful firepower in the NGS role. The large superstructure block contains adequate space for command facilities and consequently both vessels are fitted as flagships, Shirane for Escort Flotilla One based at Yokosuka and Kuruma for Escort Flotilla Two at Sasebo. Approximately 20 command staff are embarked in addition to the normal ship's complement. The two Haruna class DDHs are employed as flagships for Escort Flotillas Three and Four.

Haruna (DDH-141), ASW destroyer. Shirane class destroyers are similar but can be distinguished by their twin funnels. (Guy Toremans)

SPECIFICATION

Type: DDG
Class: Shirane/Haruna
Displacement: 5,200 tons standard
Length: 521.5ft (159m)
Beam: 57.5ft (17.5m)
Draught: 17.5ft (5.3m)
Machinery: 2 boilers, 2 IHI turbines, 70,000hp; 2 shafts
Speed & Range: 31kt
Complement: 360 + staff
Missiles: 1 Mk.25 octuple launcher, Sea Sparrow short-range SAM
Guns: 2 FMC Mk.42 5in (127mm)/54 automatic; 2 Vulcan/Phalanx 6-barrelled 20mm CIWS
ASW & USW: 2 Mk.68 triple 324mm (12.75in) torpedo tubes, Mk.46 A/S torpedoes; Prairie Masker noise suppression system
Sensors: radar: OPS-12 long-range 3D air search; OPS-28 surface search; OFS-2D navigation; WM25 and Type 72-1A fire control; sonar: SQS-35J medium-frequency search and attack VDS; OQS 101 bow-mounted; SQR-18A passive towed array
Aircraft: 3 SH-60J helicopters

THE NETHERLANDS
DDG, De Zeven Provincien

THESE LARGE DESTROYERS CONTINUE The Netherlands' record of designing and building innovative and successful warships. Carrying a powerful missile armament, their prime role is area air defence using the American-built Standard SM-2 surface-to-air missile backed up by a state-of-the-art multi-function radar system designed and built in Holland. At one time a collaborative programme with Germany and Spain was envisaged but conflicting national requirements led to the break-up of any formal consortium. However, there remains some significant commonality of equipment, particularly with the German Type 124 frigate which uses the same air defence system based on the Standard SM-2MR and Evolved Sea Sparrow missiles, and also has the same sonar suite and much radar and electronic equipment.

The clean profile of the *De Zeven Provincien* and her sister ships is clearly intended to give these ships a stealth capability and is dominated by the faceted array of the Signaal APAR multi-function radar atop the forward superstructure. The Mk.41 VLS silo on the foredeck has 40 cells, each of which can accommodate one Standard missile or a Sea Sparrow quad pack. ASW weaponry includes two twin fixed 324mm (12.75in) torpedo tubes recessed into the faired superstructure just forward of the hangar which will initially accommodate a Westland SH-14D Lynx helicopter, although this will eventually be replaced by the NH-90 when this enters service with the *Marine Luchtvaartdienst* in 2007.

The shipbuilding programme envisages four ships (*De Zeven Provincien, De Ruyter, Tromp, Evertsen*). The first two have already been laid down and are due for completion in 2002 and 2003, when they will replace the existing *Tromp* and *De Ruyter*. The last pair are due in 2004 and 2006, and will replace the current air defence variants of the Kortenaar class frigates, *Jacob van Heemskerck* and *Witte de With*.

Impression of the De Zeven Provincien class air defence destroyers which will enter service from 2002.
(Schelde Shipbuilding)

SPECIFICATION

Type: DDG
Class: De Zeven Provincien
Displacement: 6,048 tons full load
Length: 473.1ft (144.2m)
Beam: 61.7ft (18.8m)
Draught: 17.1ft 5.2m)
Machinery: CODOG; 2 Rolls-Royce Spey gas turbines, 52,300hp; 2 Stork-Wärtsilä 16V 26ST diesels, 13,600hp; 2 shafts, cp propellers
Speed & Range: 28kt; 5,000 miles (8,050km) at 18kt
Complement: 202
Missiles: 8-cell VLS, Boeing Harpoon SSM; 40-cell Mk.41 VLS, Standard SM-2MR medium-range SAM; 8-cell VLS, Evolved Sea Sparrow short-range SAM
Guns: 1 OTO Breda 5in (127mm)/54 automatic; 2 Goalkeeper 30mm CIWS; 2 Oerlikon 20mm
ASW & USW: 2 twin fixed 324mm (12.75in) torpedo tubes, Mk.46 A/S torpedoes
Sensors: radar: Signaal SMART long-range 3D air search; Signaal APAR, air and surface search/fire control; Scout surface search
Aircraft: 1 NFH-90 or Lynx helicopter

DDG, F100 Alvaro de Bazán

THE FIRST OF FOUR PROJECTED F100 class of air defence ships was laid down at Ferrol in September 1999 and was launched early in 2001 for completion in 2002. The remaining three will enter service between 2003 and 2006.

This construction programme is in step with the Dutch De Zeven Provincien class and the German Type 124 air defence ships, and there has been considerable co-operation between the three countries. However, hopes of a common design did not reach fruition and each country has gone its own way, although some items of equipment are common. In particular, the Spanish decision to adopt the Aegis combat system and its associated AN/SPY-1D multi-function radar instead of the European APAR system was the main reason for the breakdown of a fully joint programme. Spain is only the second export customer for this sensitive equipment, the other being Japan. In order that this system could be fitted on the Spanish ships, a considerable redesign of the superstructure supporting the planar arrays had to be carried out as the F100s were too narrow to accommodate the standard system as fitted to the US Arleigh Burke class destroyers. The Mk.41 VLS, accommodating Standard SM-2MR and Evolved Sea Sparrow missiles, is common to the Spanish, Dutch and German ships, and the Block IIIA version of the Standard missile is effective to 93 miles (150km).

The first ship (F101) will be named *Alvaro de Bazán* and the others will be *Roger de Lauria* (F102), *Blas de Lezo* (F103) and *Méndez Núñez* (F104). When in service, these ships will replace the five Baleares class frigates which were based on the US Navy's Knox class frigates and were completed between 1973 and 1976.

Aegis-equipped F100 class air defence frigate. (Bazán)

SPECIFICATION

Type: DDG
Class: F100
Displacement: 5,800 tons full load
Length: 481.3ft (146.7m)
Beam: 57.4ft (17.5m)
Draught: 16.1ft (4.9m)
Machinery: CODOG; 2 LM2500 gas turbines, 47,328hp; 2 Bazán/Caterpillar diesels, 12,240hp; 2 shafts, cp propellers
Speed & Range: 28kt; 4,500 miles (7,240km) at 18kt
Complement: 229
Missiles: 2 quadruple fixed launchers, Boeing Harpoon long-range SSM; 48-cell Mk.41 VLS, Standard SM-2MR medium-range and Evolved Sea Sparrow short-range SAM
Guns: 1 FMC 5in (127mm)/54 Mk.45 automatic; 1 Meroka 20mm CIWS; 2 single Oerlikon 20mm
ASW & USW: 2 twin 324mm (12.75in) fixed torpedo tubes, Mk.46 A/S torpedoes; SLQ-25A Nixie towed decoy
Sensors: radar: Aegis SPY-1D/F multi-function long-range air and surface search; SPS-67 (RAN 12S) surface search; Mk.99 fire control; sonar: DE1160LF hull-mounted medium-frequency search and attack; ATAS active towed (option)
Aircraft: 1 SH-70L Seahawk LAMPS III helicopter

FFG, Sachsen (Type 124)

Artist's impression of the Type 124 Sachsen class air defence frigate.
(Blohm und Voss GmbH)

THIS FOLLOW-ON DESIGN to the Brandenburg class is a specialised AAW ship which will replace the ageing Lütjens class destroyers based on the US Charles F. Adams class and which have now been in service for over 30 years. The new F124 results from an international collaborative programme which initially included Spain and The Netherlands. The Spanish Navy decided to withdraw and concentrate on the Aegis-equipped F100 class, but the German F124 and the Dutch De Zeven Provincien classes share a common AAW system based around the Standard and Evolved Sea Sparrow missiles, and the Signaal APAR multi-function radar.

The hull of the F124 frigate is based on that of the preceding F123 class but only a single LM2500 gas turbine is installed, but more powerful twin diesels are fitted to compensate. Speed and range characteristics are very similar in both types. The 32-cell Mk.41 VLS silo is positioned just forward of the bridge and the forward superstructure is dominated by the bulk of the fixed phased array antenna of the Signaal APAR radar. Amidships, the A/S torpedoes are discharged from a trainable Mk.32 tubes instead of the internal fixed tubes of the Brandenburgs. The hangar carries the squat antenna of the SMART-L radar and will be able to accommodate two NFH-90 helicopters when these enter service around 2005. In the meantime, a pair of sonar-equipped Westland Lynx Mk.88As will be embarked initially.

Sachsen, the lead F124, was launched in November 1999 and is due to be completed in 2002. The second and third ships, *Hamburg* and *Hessen*, will be laid down in 2001 and 2002, for completion in 2004 and 2005 respectively.

SPECIFICATION

Type: FFG
Class: Sachsen (Type 124)
Displacement: 5,600 tons full load
Length: oa 469.2ft (143m)
Beam: 57.1ft (17.4m)
Draught: 24.4ft (7.4m)
Machinery: CODOG; 1 GE LM2500SA-ML gas turbine, 31,500hp; 2 MTU 20V 1163 TB93 diesels, 20,100hp; 2 shafts, cp propellers
Speed & Range: 29kt; 4,000 miles (6,440km) at 18kt
Complement: 255
Missiles: 2 fixed quadruple launchers, Boeing Harpoon SSM. 32-cell Mk.41 VLS, Standard SM-2 Block IIIA long-range SSM, Evolved Sea Sparrow short-range SAM; 2 21-cell Mk.49 launchers RAM very-short-range SAM
Guns: 1 OTO Melera 3in (76mm) automatic gun; 2 single Mauser 27mm guns
ASW & USW: 2 triple 324mm (12.75in) Mk.32 torpedo tubes, Mk.46 or Eurotorp Mu90 A/S torpedoes
Sensors: radar: SMART-L long-range 3D; Signaal APAR multi-function phased array; Triton-G surface search; I-band navigation; sonar: Atlas DSQS-24B medium-frequency search and attack; provision for towed array
Aircraft: 2 helicopters

DDG, Iroquois

HMCS **Huron** *(DD-281), Iroquois class air defence ship. (Canadian Armed Forces)*

THIS CLASS OF FOUR DESTROYERS WAS originally laid down in 1969 and completed in 1972/73. As built, their armament comprised a single 5in (127mm) gun, Sea Sparrow surface-to-air missiles, a Limbo A/S mortar and triple A/S torpedo tubes, as well as two Sea King helicopters in a large hangar amidships. A distinguishing recognition feature was the split funnel with the stacks angled outwards to either side. By the 1990s the ships' anti-submarine armament was outdated and this role was being better executed by the new Halifax class frigates then coming into service. It was therefore decided that the Iroquois class destroyers should be modernised and rebuilt as dedicated air defence ships, and this process became the Tribal class Update and Modernisation Project (TRUMP).

The ASW armament remained unchanged except that the Limbo mortar was removed, but the major change was the deletion of the forward 5in (127mm) gun and its replacement by a US Mk.41 VLS set into the foredeck. This housed 32 Standard SM-2 surface-to-air missiles and new search and fire control radars were installed as part of the upgrade. A single OTO Melera 3in (76mm) automatic gun was mounted in front of the bridge and a Vulcan/Phalanx CIWS atop the hangar. Two CH-124 Sea King ASW helicopters can be accommodated, although only one at a time can operate on the flightdeck which is positioned well forward of the stern for minimum pitch characteristics in a seaway.

Algonquin was the first ship to undergo the TRUMP refit, commencing in November 1987 and completing in October 1991. The remaining three were modernised between 1988 and January 1995. Since that date further improvements have been made to the sonar outfit, communications equipment and EW systems. As modernised, these ships have a purposeful appearance and the Standard missile system makes them extremely effective in the AAW role. Two ships are normally based on the Pacific coast and the other pair on the eastern seaboard.

HMCS **Athabaskan** *(DD-282), showing twin hangars. (D. Hannaford)*

SPECIFICATION

Type: DDG
Class: Iroquois
Displacement: 5,300 tons full load
Length: 426ft (129.8m)
Beam: 50ft (15.2m)
Draught: hull 15.5ft (4.7m)
Machinery: COGOG; 2 P&W FT4A2 gas turbines, 50,000hp; 2 Allison 570-KF gas turbines, 12,700hp; 2 shafts, cp propellers
Speed & Range: 27kt; 4,500 miles (7,240km) at 15kt
Complement: 292
Missiles: Mk.41 multi-cell VLS, Standard SM-2MR long-range SAM
Guns: 1 OTO Melera 3in (76mm)/62 automatic; 1 Vulcan/Phalanx 6-barrelled 20mm CIWS
ASW & USW: 2 Mk.32 triple 324mm (12.75in) torpedo tubes, Mk.46 torpedoes; SLQ-25 Nixie torpedo decoy
Sensors: radar: SPQ-502 (Signaal LW08) long-range air search; SPQ-501 (DW08) surface search; SPG-501 (STIR 1.8) fire control; Pathfinder navigation; sonar: SQS-510 combined hull-mounted and VDS, active search and attack
Aircraft: 2 helicopters

DDG, Murasame

THESE LARGE DESTROYERS are sophisticated anti-submarine platforms with a strong surface action capability. For air defence only the short-range Sea Sparrow is fitted although two Vulcan/Phalanx CIWS provide an effective back-up. The main ASW weapon is the ASROC torpedo carrying missile which is housed in a 16-cell launcher on the foredeck, although a total of 29 missiles can be stowed onboard. Triple torpedo tubes are located on either beam amidships and these fire the standard Mk.46 homing torpedo. These are also carried by the single SH-60J helicopter, which is a sophisticated ASW weapon system in its own right.

The name ship commissioned in 1996, and four were in service by the end of 1999 (*Murasame, Harusame, Yuudachi, Kirisame*). Two more were completed in 2000 (*Inazuma* and *Samidare*), and a total of nine will be completed by 2002. The construction programme has been given added impetus due to the decision not to build any further Kongo class destroyers and consequently two more ships, laid down in May 2000, will be completed as Improved Murasame class. These will carry an OTO Breda 5in (127mm) gun which will replace the previous 3in (76mm) Compact, and a Mk.41 VLS capable of carrying more Sea Sparrow missiles instead of the existing Mk.48 VLS. An improved sonar will also be fitted, and the installation of the Mk.41 VLS may indicate the possibility of upgrading to Standard SM-2 missiles in the future, although this would require a major upgrade of the radars and fire control systems.

Harusame (DD-102). A Murasame class DDG of the JMSDF.
(Department of Defence)

SPECIFICATIONS

Type: DDG
Class: Murasame
Displacement: 4,550 tons standard, 5,100 tons full load
Length: 495.4ft (151m)
Beam: 57.1ft (17.4m)
Draught: 17.1ft (5.2m)
Machinery: COGAG; 2 Rolls-Royce Spey SM1C gas turbines, 41,630hp; 2 LM2500 gas turbines, 43,000hp; 2 shafts
Speed & Range: 30kt
Complement: 166
Missiles: 2 quadruple fixed launchers, Boeing Harpoon SSM; Mk.48 16-cell VLS, Sea Sparrow short-range SAM
Guns: 1 OTO Melera 3in (76mm)/62 automatic gun; 2 Vulcan/Phalanx 6-barrelled 20mm CIWS
ASW & USW: Mk.41 16-cell VLS, ASROC A/S missile system; 2 triple Type 68 324mm (12.75in) torpedo tubes, Mk.46 A/S torpedoes
Sensors: Melco OPS-24 long-range 3D air search; OPS-28D surface search; OPS-20 navigation; Type 2-31 fire control; sonar: OQS-5 hull-mounted low-frequency active search and attack; OQR-1 passive towed array
Aircraft: 1 helicopter (SH-60J Seahawk)

DDG, De La Penne

Francesco Mimbelli *(D561).*
(author)

THESE TWO HEAVILY ARMED destroyers, *Luigi Durand de la Penne* and *Francesco Mimbelli*, were ordered in 1986 and laid down in 1988 and 1989 respectively. They were originally to be named *Animoso* and *Ardimentoso*, but these names were changed in 1992 prior to the ships' completion in 1993.

Of typical racy Italian outline, these ships deploy the Standard SM-1MR medium-range SAM to provide an air defence umbrella for accompanying task forces, and the Teseo anti-ship missile gives a long-range striking power. A heavy emphasis is placed on the gun armament. The forward 5in (127mm) gun in each of these ships was taken from the earlier Audace class ships, which originally carried two such weapons but one was removed and replaced by a surface-to-air missile system in 1988. The OTO Melera 3in (76mm) Super Rapid guns can fire 120 rounds per minute over a distance of 10 miles (16km). The proximity fused shells with a fragmentation warhead have a good chance of destroying small targets such as anti-ship missiles without having to achieve a direct hit.

In recent years the Italian Navy has been involved in several operations outside the traditional Mediterranean theatre and to support these deployments a force of four large destroyers is maintained, the balance being made up by the two Audace class ships which were completed in 1972. At 3,600 tons displacement, they are slightly smaller than the De La Pennes although carrying a similar armament. Their replacements will eventually be the Aster missile-armed Project Horizon frigates, now a joint Franco–Italian programme following the UK's withdrawal in 1999.

SPECIFICATION

Type: DDG
Class: De La Penne
Displacement: 4,330 tons standard, 5,400 tons full load
Length: 487.4ft (147.7m)
Beam: 52.8ft (16.1m)
Draught: 28.2ft (8.6m) inc. sonar dome
Machinery: CODOG; 2 Fiat GE LM2500 gas turbines, 54,000hp; 2 GMT BL230.20 DVM diesels, 12,600hp; 2 shafts, cp propellers
Speed & Range: 31 kt; 7,000 miles (11,260km) at 18kt
Complement: 377
Missiles: 2 or 4 twin launchers, OTO Melera/Matra Teseo Mk.2 long-range SSM; 1 Mk.13 Mod 4 launcher, Standard SM-1MR medium-range SAM
Guns: 1 OTO Melera 5in (127mm) automatic gun; 3 OTO Melera 3in (76mm)/62 Super Rapid automatic guns
ASW & USW: 2 triple B-515 324mm (12.75in) torpedo tubes, Mk.46 A/S torpedoes; SLQ-25 Nixie torpedo decoy
Sensors: radar: Hughes SPS-52C long-range 3D air search; Selenia SPS-768 air search; Selenia SPS-774 air and surface search; SMA SPS-702 surface search; Selenia SPG-76 and Raytheon SPG-51D fire control; SMA SPN-748 navigation; sonar: Raytheon DE1164 LF-VDS medium-frequency active search and attack comprising integrated bow and VDS systems
Aircraft: 2 helicopters

Francesco Mimbelli, *midships section.*
(author)

FRANCE
DDG, Cassard (Type F70)

THIS CLASS OF TWO SHIPS was completed in 1988 (*Cassard*) and 1991 (*Jean Bart*). They are based on the preceding Georges Leygues class but differ mainly in that they carry the US Standard SM-1MR medium-range surface-to-air missile system for area defence. The launchers for these were taken from stricken vessels of the T47 Surcouf class, which had been armed with the US Terrier missile. Future plans are for the two Cassard class ships to be armed with the Aster 30 SAM currently under development.

These ships also differ from the earlier ships in that the propulsion system is entirely diesel-based as opposed to the CODOG installation in the F70 class. The diesel exhausts are trunked up into a squat structure amidships which also carries the dome enclosing the DRBJ 11B radar atop the funnel. Immediately abaft of this are the two Raytheon SPG-51C target-tracking radars for the Standard missiles which are fired from a single arm launcher mounted just forward of the hangar.

A single AS 565MA Panther helicopter is carried and its main role is to provide targeting information for the Exocet MM40 anti-ship missiles which have a range of 40 miles (70km). Although initially rated as destroyers, they are now classified as F70 FAA (*Frégates Anti-Aériennes*) although still carrying the destroyer pennant numbers D614 (*Cassard*) and D615 (*Jean Bart*). Two other ships were originally ordered in 1984 but were subsequently cancelled and the existing two are due to decommission in 2013

Jean Bart, *Cassard class destroyer.*
(Marine Nationale, France)

and 2015, although they will undergo mid-life modernisation refits in 2003/4 during which the obsolescent Standard SM-1MR missiles will be replaced.

France, along with Italy, is continuing with the Horizon class air defence ships. The first two are expected to enter service in 2005 and 2007.

FNS Cassard, *Type F70 air defence destroyer.*
(Marine Nationale, France)

SPECIFICATION

Type: DDG
Class: Cassard (Type F70)
Displacement: 4,230 tons standard, 4,730 tons full load
Length: 455.9ft (139m)
Beam: 45.9ft (14m)
Draught: 21.3ft (6.5m) inc. sonar
Machinery: 4 SEMT-Pielstick 18 PA6 V280 BTC diesels, 43,200 hp; 2 shafts
Speed & Range: 29.5kt; 8,200 miles (13,200km) at 17kt
Complement: 225 (251 max.)
Missiles: 8 Exocet MM40 SSM in 2 groups of 4 launchers; 1 Mk.13 Mod 5 launcher, Standard SM-1MR medium-range SAM; 2 Matra Sadral PDMS sextuple launchers, Mistral close-in SAM
Guns: 1 3.9in (100mm)/55 CADAM automatic gun; 2 Oerlikon 20mm guns; 4 12.7mm (0.5in) machine-guns
ASW & USW: 2 fixed torpedo launchers, ECAN L5 Mod 4 A/S torpedoes; Nixie towed decoy
Sensors: radar: Thompson CSF DRBJ 11B long-range 3D air search; DRBV 26C medium-range air/surface search; Racal DRBN 34A navigation and aircraft control; Thompson CSF DRBC 33A and Raytheon SPG-51C fire control; sonar: Thompson Sintra DUBA 25A medium-frequency search and attack
Aircraft: 1 helicopter

FG, Type 22

HMS **Chatham** *(F87), Type 22 Batch III class frigate. (Royal Navy)*

A TOTAL OF 14 TYPE 22s were built for the Royal Navy in three separate groups. The original design was for a specialised ASW warship to replace the successful Leander class frigates dating back to the 1960s. The result was a much larger ship which had the distinction of being the first Royal Navy ship without a gun as part of the main armament. The first four (*Broadsword, Battleaxe, Brilliant* and *Brazen*) commissioned between 1979 and 1982 and some saw service in the Falklands War, where their Seawolf missile systems proved to be extremely effective. All have now been retired and sold to Brazil.

The second batch (*Boxer, Beaver, Brave, London, Sheffield, Coventry*) entered service between 1984 and 1988, the last two being named after Type 42 destroyers lost in the Falklands. Compared to the earlier ships, Batch II featured a lengthened hull and introduced the Type 2031 TAS, and the last four also had Rolls-Royce SM1 Spey engines as the main propulsion plant instead of the Olympus TM.3B used in all previous Type 22s. Currently only *Sheffield* and *Coventry* remain in service, with the others laid up for disposal.

The last four Batch III ships (*Cornwall, Chatham, Cumberland, Campbeltown*) were a considerable advance and incorporated many of the lessons learnt in the Falklands. Based on the lengthened hull introduced in the Batch II ships, they mounted a 4.5in (115mm) automatic gun on the foredeck and carried Harpoon SSMs instead of the shorter-range Exocets. For short-range defence against missiles and aircraft, a Goalkeeper CIWS was mounted high up on the forward superstructure. The Seawolf GWS-25 missile system was enhanced by the introduction of Type 911 tracking radars, and a GSA 8B Sea Archer optronic director using infra-red and TV tracking was fitted for use with both Seawolf and the 4.5in (115mm) gun. Finally, the after hangar and flightdeck was enlarged to enable these ships to operate a Merlin HM.1 ASW helicopter instead of the two Lynxes, which was the normal aircraft complement of all Type 22s. Taken together, these changes have made the Batch III Type 22s extremely powerful and effective general-purpose warships.

HMS **Cornwall** *(F99), the first of four Type 22 Batch III frigates. (Royal Navy)*

SPECIFICATION

Type: FG
Class: Type 22
Displacement: 4,200 tons standard, 4,900 tons full load
Length: 485.9ft (148.1m)
Beam: 48.5ft (14.8m)
Draught: 21ft (6.4m)
Machinery: COGOG; 2 Rolls-Royce Spey SM1A gas turbines, 29,500hp; 2 Rolls-Royce RM3C Tyne gas turbines, 10,680hp; 2 shafts, cp propellers
Speed & Range: 30kt; 4,500 miles (7,240km) at 18kt
Complement: 250 (301 max.)
Missiles: 2 fixed quadruple launchers, Boeing Harpoon long-range SSM; 2 GWS-25 sextuple launchers, Seawolf short-range SAM
Guns: 1 Vickers 4.5in (115mm)/55 Mk.8 automatic gun; 1 Goalkeeper 30mm CIWS; 2 DS30B single 30mm guns
ASW & USW: 2 STWS Mk.2 triple 324mm (12.75in) torpedo tubes, Stingray A/S torpedoes; Type 182 or SLQ-25A torpedo decoys
Sensors: radar: Marconi Type 967/968 medium-range air and surface search; Type 1007 navigation; Marconi Type 911 fire control; sonar: Type 2050 active search and attack; Type 2031 passive towed array
Aircraft: 2 helicopters (max.)

HMS **Campbeltown** *(F86) at anchor. (author)*

FFG, Brandenburg (Type 123)

ORIGINALLY KNOWN AS the Deutschland class, these four large frigates (*Brandenburg, Schleswig-Holstein, Bayern, Mecklenburg-Vorpommern*) were laid down in 1992/93 and subsequently commissioned between 1994 and 1996. The overall design is similar to that of the very successful MEKO frigates built for export, but features the same propulsion system as the preceding Bremen class. At 4,900 tons full load they are much larger, and the hull is almost 30ft (9m) longer. The weather deck is raised by one level compared to the F122 class, and this gives a considerable increase in internal volume to improve habitability and to provide much enlarged operational spaces. So, for example, the spacious and well-equipped CIC has an additional compartment alongside with almost identical equipment for use by a task group command staff if required.

Despite this increase in size, armament remains very similar, and in fact the Exocet MM38 missiles carried by the F123 class have a range of only 26 miles (42km) compared with 81 miles (130km) for the Harpoon missiles on the earlier ships. The Exocets and their launchers were taken from the three Hamburg class destroyers which were laid up prior to the F123 class commissioning. Two 21-cell RAM launchers are carried, one forward of the bridge and the other on the hangar roof. The large twin hangar and flightdeck will be able to accommodate the NH-90 helicopter, although two Westland Lynx Mk.88As are currently embarked. A passive TAS will be fitted in the near future to supplement the bow-mounted active DSQS-23BZ sonar and the Lynxes are fitted with AQS-18 dipping sonar. The main shipboard ASW weapons are the Mk.46 or DM 4A1 homing torpedoes which are fired from fixed tubes located within the hull just forward of the hangar. An automated magazine system allows for rapid reloading.

Schleswig-Holstein *(F216), Brandenburg class Type 123 frigate. (German Navy)*

Bayern *(F217), Brandenburg class Type 123 frigate. (German Navy)*

Brandenburg *(F215), Type 123 frigate. (German Navy)*

SPECIFICATION

Type: FFG
Class: Brandenburg (Type 123)
Displacement: 4,900 tons full load
Length: oa 455.7ft (138.9m), wl 416.3ft (126.9m)
Beam: 54.8ft (16.7m)
Draught: 22.3ft (6.8m)
Machinery: CODOG; 2 GE LM2500SA-ML gas turbines, 51,000hp; 2 MTU 20V 956 TB92 diesels, 11,070hp; 2 shafts, cp propellers
Speed & Range: 29kt (18kt on diesels); 4,000 miles (6,440km) at 18kt
Complement: 218
Missiles: 2 twin launchers, Exocet MM38 medium-range SSM; 16-cell Mk.41 VLS, Sea Sparrow short-range SAM; 2 21-cell Mk.49 launchers, RAM short-range SAM
Guns: 1 OTO Melera 3in (76mm) automatic gun; 2 single 20mm or 27mm guns
ASW & USW: 2 twin 324mm (12.75in) fixed torpedo tubes, Mk.46 A/S torpedoes
Sensors: radar: Signaal LW08 long-range air search; Signaal SMART 3D air and surface search; Signaal STIR 180 fire control/tracking; Raytheon Raypath navigation; sonar: Atlas DSQS-23BZ medium-frequency search and attack; provision for towed array but not fitted
Aircraft: 2 helicopters

FFH, Halifax

CANADA BUILT A SERIES of very seaworthy and efficient ASW frigates in the 1950s and 1960s, but two decades later they were urgently in need of replacement. Following a hard-fought international competition, a contract to build six new Halifax class frigates was won by St John Shipbuilding in 1983 with a follow-up order for another six being placed in 1987. Three ships of the original order were subcontracted to Marine Industries and the lead ship, HMCS *Halifax*, was laid down in March 1987 at St John's New Brunswick and subsequently commissioned in June 1992. The whole class was completed by 1996 with the last ship, HMCS *Ottawa*, commissioning on 28 September of that year.

At 4,770 tons full load, these are quite large frigates and easily distinguished by the large square funnel amidships housing the uptakes for the two gas turbines and single diesel engine, intended to reduce IR emissions from these sources. A single large hangar is provided to house a CH-124 Sea King helicopter. An interesting feature of these ships is the fitting of a Bofors 57mm (2.2in) gun, capable of firing 20 rounds per minute, as the main gun armament. This is considerably lighter than the ordnance usually fitted to ships of this size but it does have the advantage of a very high rate of fire and is probably more effective in the anti-aircraft role, although less suitable for NGS purposes.

Currently, the Canadian Maritime Command maintains two standing task forces, each comprising an Iroquois class DDG, two Halifax class frigates and a Victoria class submarine. The other frigates are allocated to routine tasks as well as training and refitting. The possibility of converting up to four Halifax frigates to AAW ships is being considered, and changes would include a new multi-function radar and Standard and Evolved Sea Sparrow SAMs, probably launched from a VLS silo. If such conversions were carried out, they would probably replace the four Iroquois class destroyers which are currently almost 30 years old.

HMCS* Vancouver *(331), Halifax class frigate. (Canadian Armed Forces)

SPECIFICATION

Type: FFH
Class: Halifax
Displacement: 4,770 tons full load
Length: oa 441.9ft (134.7m), pp 408.5ft (124.5m)
Beam: 53.8ft (16.4m)
Draught: 16.4ft (5m)
Machinery: CODOG; 2 GE LM2500 gas turbines, 47,500hp; 1 SEMT-Pielstick 20 PA6 V280 diesel, 8,800hp; 2 shafts
Speed & Range: 29kt; 9,500 miles (15,300km) at 13kt
Complement: 215 (inc. air detachment)
Missiles: 2 quadruple launchers, Boeing Harpoon Block 1C SSM; 2 Mk.48 octuple launchers, Sea Sparrow SAM
Guns: 1 Bofors 57mm (2.2in)/70 Mk.2; 1 20mm Vulcan/Phalanx CIWS; 8 12.7mm (0.5in) machine-guns
ASW & USW: 2 twin Mk.32 324mm (12.75in) torpedo tubes, Mk.46 A/S torpedoes; Nixie SLQ-25 towed acoustic decoy
Sensors: radar: Raytheon SPS-49(V)5 long-range air search; Ericsson Sea Giraffe HC150 medium-range surface/air search; Signaal SPG-503/STIR fire control; Kelvin Hughes Type 1007 navigation; sonar: Westinghouse SQS-510 hull-mounted medium-frequency search and attack; CDC SQR-501 CANTASS towed array
Aircraft: 1 helicopter

HMCS* Calgary *(335), Halifax class frigate. (Canadian Armed Forces)

DDG, Georges Leygues (Type F70)

Georges Leygues, *Type F70 ASW destroyer.* *(Marine Nationale, France)*

ALTHOUGH ALLOCATED DESTROYER pennant numbers, these seven ships with their comprehensive ASW suite and lack of an area air defence missile system would more likely be classified as frigates in other navies (in fact, they were reclassified as such in 1988, now being termed F70 FASM – *Frégates Anti Sous-Marins*). All seven ships were built at Brest Naval Dockyard and were laid down between 1974 and 1984 for completion from 1979 to 1990. Apart from the name ship, the others are *Dupleix* (completed 1981), *Montcalm* (1982), *Jean de Vienne* (1984), *Primauguet* (1986), *La Motte-Picquet* (1988) and *La Touche-Tréville* (1990).

The ASW capability is enhanced by the two embarked Lynx helicopters which are sonar-equipped. Air defence capability relies on the Crotale SAM system which has a range of only 8 miles (13km), although this can be supplemented by the Mistral very-short-range infra-red homing SAM with a range of 2.5 miles (4km). These can be fired from the Simbad twin launcher, which replaces the 20mm guns. The first four ships have just completed an air defence upgrade which involves the replacement of the old 20mm Oerlikons with modern rapid-fire 30mm guns and the mounting of two Sadral six rail launchers for Mistral missiles atop the forward superstructure. In addition there is a new air search radar and a command bridge has been installed above the existing navigation bridge. An ASW upgrade is also planned which will include a new lightweight TAS, although plans to fit the Franco–Italian Milas ASW missile have been dropped.

SPECIFICATION

Type: DDG
Class: Georges Leygues (Type F70)
Displacement: 3,850 tons standard, up to 4,580 tons full load
Length: 455.9ft (139m)
Beam: 45.9ft (14m)
Draught: 18.7ft (5.7m)
Machinery: CODOG; 2 Rolls-Royce TM3B Olympus gas turbines, 46,200hp; 2 SEMT-Pielstick 16 PA6 V280 diesels, 12,800hp; 2 shafts, cp propellers
Speed & Range: 30kt; 8,500 miles (13,680km) at 18kt
Complement: 218
Missiles: 4 single launchers, MM38 Exocet SAM; 1 octuple launcher, short-range Crotale SAM Matra Simbad twin launchers or Matra Sadral sextuple launchers fitted in some ships
Guns: 1 3.9in (100mm)/55 CADAM automatic gun; 2 Oerlikon 20mm guns (or 2 Breda/Mauser 30mm when modernised)
ASW & USW: 2 fixed launchers, ECAN L5 A/S torpedoes
Sensors: radar: Thompson CSF DRBV 26 long-/medium-range air search (modernised ships); Thompson CSF DRBV 51A or 51C medium-range air/surface search; Decca 1226 navigation and aircraft control; Thompson CSF Vega with DRBC 32E or 33A fire control; sonar: Thompson Sintra DUBV 24C active search and attack; DUBV 43B VDS; DUBV23/24 towed array
Aircraft: 2 helicopters

DG, Type 42

THE TYPE 42 DESTROYER was designed specifically to deploy the Sea Dart missile in order to provide an effective area air defence system for the Royal Navy following the cancellation of the CVA-01 carriers in the mid-1960s. The lead ship, HMS *Sheffield*, was laid down in 1970 and commissioned in 1975, while a further five (*Birmingham*, *Cardiff*, *Glasgow*, *Newcastle*, *Coventry*) were completed by the end of 1979. Two identical ships were also built for export to Argentina – a rather unfortunate sale in view of events a few years later.

The Batch I Type 42s were followed by a further four Batch II ships (*Exeter*, *Southampton*, *Nottingham*, *Liverpool*) which differed mainly in that they were equipped with the more capable Type 1022 long-range radar instead of the Type 965 originally carried. In the 1982 Falklands War the Type 42s with their Sea Dart missiles provided a significant proportion of the Royal Navy's air defence assets, although in the fierce fighting two ships, *Sheffield* and *Coventry*, were lost in action. As a result of experiences in the Falklands all Type 42s were modified and initially given a more effective close-range armament in the form of modern GAM-BO1 20mm guns and GCM-AO3 twin 30mm mountings to supplement or replace the original Oerlikon 20mm Mk.7A.

Too late to see service in the Falklands were four Batch III ships (*Manchester*, *Gloucester*, *Edinburgh* and *York*) which commissioned between 1982 and 1985. These were similar to the preceding ships except for a lengthened bow which gave them a more pleasing appearance and improved seaworthiness.

From 1987 onwards, a Vulcan/Phalanx CIWS replaced the twin 30mm mountings on either side of the funnel but a plan to fit a lightweight Seawolf missile system was dropped in 1991. All Type 42s carry a Lynx helicopter which is armed with Sea Skua anti-ship missiles as well as ASW homing torpedoes, the latter dropped under the direction of the mother ship as the Lynx is not sonar-equipped.

As the first of the Type 42s commissioned in the mid-1970s, their replacement is becoming a matter of some urgency. The planned successor was an air defence version of the international Project Horizon frigate, but this failed to materialise as the various countries involved could not agree on some of

HMS Edinburgh (D97), Type 42 Batch III destroyer. (author)

the most important parameters, including the specification of the all-important missile system and associated radar equipment. Britain is now proceeding with a national solution in the shape of the Type 45 destroyer project. This will be a 6,000-ton ship armed with the new principal anti-air missile system (PAAMS), the main elements of which are the Aster 15 or 30 missile, a 48-cell Sylver VLS and the Sampson multi-function radar. In order to replace the Batch II and III Type 42s as they retire, the first Type 45 will need to be ready by 2007 at the latest.

SPECIFICATION

Type: DG
Class: Type 42
Displacement: 3,500 tons standard, 4,675 tons full load
Length: 462.8ft (141.1m)
Beam: 49ft (14.9m)
Draught: 19ft (5.8m)
Machinery: COGOG; 2 Rolls-Royce Olympus TM3B Olympus gas turbines, 43,000hp; 2 Rolls-Royce RM1C Tyne gas turbines, 10,680hp; 2 shafts, cp propellers
Speed & Range: 30kt; 4,000 miles (6,440km) at 18kt
Complement: 301
Missiles: 1 twin launcher, Sea Dart medium-range SAM
Guns: 1 Vickers 4.5in (115mm)/55 Mk.8 automatic gun; 4 single 20mm guns (GAM-B01 or Oerlikon); 2 Vulcan/Phalanx 20mm CIWS
ASW & USW: 2 STWS Mk.2 triple 324mm (12.75in) torpedo tubes, Stingray A/S torpedoes; Type 182 or SLQ-25A torpedo decoys
Sensors: radar: Type 1022 long-range air search; Plessey Type 996 medium-range air and surface search; Type 1007 and Type 1008 navigation; Marconi Type 909 fire control
Aircraft: 1 helicopter
(Note: data applies to Batch III ships)

CHINA
DDG, Luhu

THESE TWO SHIPS, *Haribing* and *Qingdao*, were completed in 1994 and 1996 respectively and can be regarded as China's first really modern destroyers. The lead ship was powered by US-supplied LM2500 gas turbines while the second was fitted with Ukrainian-designed units. There is a strong French influence with radars, sonars and the Crotale missile system all coming from that source, while the Harbin Zhi-9A Haitun helicopter is a Chinese-manufactured version of the Eurocopter/Aérospatiale Dauphin 2. The C-801 and C-802 surface-to-surface missiles are of Chinese design and manufacture and have ranges of 25 miles (40km) and 75 miles (120km) respectively, the latter being broadly similar to the Harpoon missile which is widely used by Western navies. Considerable emphasis is placed on self-defence with the Crotale missile system and the four radar-directed twin 37mm guns providing a good close-in defence through all quadrants.

The first ship was ordered in 1985 but the construction programme was drawn out while export orders for Thailand were given a higher priority. In 1996 the first of two follow-on vessels was laid down and was commissioned in 1999. Based on the Luhu design, the new Luhai class ships are just over 30ft (9m) longer with standard displacement rising to 6,000 tons. A similar armament is carried except that the SSM battery comprises 16 C-802 missiles and the twin 37mm guns are all grouped around the hangar aft. The most obvious external difference is the introduction of a second funnel between the mainmast and hangar.

**Haribing *(112), one of two Luhu Type 052 class destroyers of the PLAN.
(US Navy)***

SPECIFICATION

Type: DDG
Class: Luhu
Displacement: 4,200 tons full load
Length: 468.2ft (142.7m)
Beam: 49.5ft (15.1m)
Draught: 16.7ft (5.1m)
Machinery: CODOG; 2 LM2500 or 2 Ukraine gas turbines, 55,000/48,600hp; 2 MTU 12V 1163 TB83 diesels, 8,840hp; 2 shafts, cp propellers
Speed & Range: 31kt; 5,000 miles (8,050km) at 15kt
Complement: 230
Missiles: 4 fixed twin launchers, C-801 or C-802 SSM; 1 HQ-7 octuple launcher, Crotale short-range SAM
Guns: 1 twin 3.9in (100mm)/56; 4 twin 37mm /63
ASW & USW: 2 triple BS15 324mm (12.75in) torpedo tubes, Yu-2/Mk.46 A/S torpedoes
Sensors: radar: Hai Ying air search; TSR3004 Sea Tiger air and surface search; China ESR1 surface search; Racal Decca 1229 navigation, Type 347G, EFR1 Rice Lamp and Castor II fire control; sonar: DUBV-23 hull-mounted medium-frequency active search and attack; DUBV-43 medium-frequency active VDS
Aircraft: 2 helicopters

FG, Duke (Type 23)

HMS *NORFOLK*, THE LEAD SHIP of the class, was launched in 1987 and commissioned in 1990. It was followed by a further 15 ships of which the last, HMS *St Albans*, will be completed in mid-2002. At one time it was hoped that more would be ordered, but even a total of 16 makes it the largest class of British post-war frigates apart from the Leander class (26 ships).

Originally intended as a cheap replacement for the large and complex Type 22 frigates, the Duke class eventually matured into a sophisticated general-purpose frigate with substantial anti-surface ship and anti-submarine capabilities. The hangar and flightdeck were designed to accommodate the Merlin HM.1 helicopter which entered service from late 1999 onwards, although a Lynx HMA.3/8 is normally embarked pending the availability of the larger machine. Virtually all the armament is concentrated on the foredeck, making these ships vulnerable to being disabled by a single hit. The main exception is the internal magazine torpedo launch system (MTLS) which is located in the forward section of the hangar superstructure. This enables the twin torpedo tubes to be reloaded with Stingray ASW torpedoes in less than 10 minutes. The design incorporates some stealth technology intended to reduce the ships' IR and acoustic signatures, while the shape of the hull and superstructure reduces radar echoes.

The complexity of modern weapon systems demands a sophisticated computerised combat data and command system. The original CACS-4 system specified for the Type 23 proved to be unsuitable for the task and was cancelled in 1987 in favour of the SSCS (surface ship command system). However, this took some time to develop and consequently it was not available for installation until the eighth ship, HMS *Westminster*, which commissioned in 1994. In the meantime the earlier ships had to do without an integrated system and consequently were not available for deployment in the 1991 Gulf War. SSCS is now being retrofitted to all these ships while subsequent Type 23s have the upgraded Phase III, IV or V SSCS.

HMS Westminster (F237) showing concentration of armament on the forecastle.
(Royal Navy)

HMS Somerset (F82), Type 23 Duke class frigate.
(author)

SPECIFICATION

Type: FG
Class: Duke (Type 23)
Displacement: 3,500 tons standard, 4,200 tons full load
Length: 436.2ft (133m)
Beam: 52.8ft (16.1m)
Draught: 18ft (7.3m)
Machinery: CODLAG; 2 Rolls-Royce Spey SM1A gas turbines, 31,000hp; 4 Paxman 12CM diesels, 8,100hp; 2 GEC motors; 2 shafts
Speed & Range: 28kt; 8,980 miles (14,450km) at 15kt
Complement: 181
Missiles: 2 quadruple launchers, Boeing Harpoon long-range SSM; 32-canister VLS silo, GWS 26 Seawolf short-range SAM
Guns: 1 Vickers 4.5in (115mm)/55 Mk.8 automatic gun; 2 DS30B single 30mm guns
ASW & USW: 2 fixed twin 324mm (12.75in) torpedo tubes with automatic reload, Stingray A/S torpedoes
Sensors: radar: Type 996 3D air and surface search; Type 1007 navigation; Type 911 fire control; sonar: Type 2050 bow-mounted active search and attack; Type 2031Z passive towed array or Type 2087 towed active and passive array
Aircraft: 1 helicopter

JAPAN
DDG, Asagiri

THESE EIGHT SHIPS ARE SIMILAR in size and displacement to the British Type 42 destroyers although they were built to a slightly later timescale, commissioning between 1988 and 1991. Their design can be regarded as a stretched and improved Hatsuyuki class, of which 11 ships were built up to 1987. The obvious external difference was a longer hull and two funnels, but in other respects the two classes were very similar with an almost identical weapons fit. The earlier ships had a mix of Rolls-Royce Olympus and Tyne engines in a COGAG machinery layout, but the later Asagiris had the more flexible four-Spey installation. Although not immediately apparent from most angles, the two funnels are actually slightly offset to port and starboard while the mainmast is also offset to port. This arrangement is an attempt to reduce the effect of the hot exhaust gases on the radars and other electronic equipment on the mast. These ships originally operated Sea King ASW helicopters but these have now been replaced and both classes carry a single SH-60J Seahawk helicopter, built under licence in Japan and comprehensively equipped with radar sonar and ASW weapons including Mk.46 homing torpedoes.

Asagiri was completed in 1988, and the other ships of the class are *Yamagiri* (1989), *Yuugiri* (1989), *Amagiri* (1989), *Hamagiri* (1990), *Setogiri* (1990), *Sawagiri* (1990) and *Umigiri* (1991). The last four ships were completed with improved and updated radar systems, and a helicopter data link and retrospectively received OQR-1 passive TAS.

Asagiri (DD-151), lead ship of eight ASW destroyers. (Rolls-Royce)

SPECIFICATION

Type: DDG
Class: Asagiri
Displacement: 3,500 tons standard, 4,200 tons full load
Length: 449.4ft (137m)
Beam: 48ft (14.6m)
Draught: 14.6ft (4.5m)
Machinery: COGAG; 4 Rolls-Royce Spey gas turbines, 53,300hp; 2 shafts, cp propellers
Speed & Range: 30kt
Complement: 220
Missiles: 2 quadruple fixed launchers, Boeing Harpoon SSM; 1 octuple Mk.29 launcher, Sea Sparrow short-range SAM
Guns: 1 OTO Melera 3in (76mm)/62 automatic; 2 Vulcan/Phalanx 6-barrelled 20mm CIWS
ASW & USW: 1 Mk.112 octuple launcher, ASROC; 2 triple Type 68 324mm (12.75in) torpedo tubes, Mk.46 A/S torpedoes
Sensors: radar: OPS-14D or OPS-24 3D long-range air search; OPS-28C surface search; Type 2-22, Type 2-12E/12G fire control; sonar: OQS-4A hull-mounted low-frequency search and attack; OQR-1 passive towed array
Aircraft: 1 helicopter

DDG, Okpo

King Kwanggaeto (971), lead ship of three KDX-1 Okpo class destroyers.
(Guy Toremans)

SOUTH KOREA IS ONE OF THE WORLD'S leading builders of merchant ships and has steadily sought to increase its expertise in naval construction. In the 10 years between 1983 and 1993, a class of 24 1,200-ton corvettes were built and nine Ulsan class 2,000-ton frigates were also completed over a similar period. With the experience gained from these programmes, a 3,500-ton destroyer programme was started in the late 1980s under the designation Project KDX-1. The gestation period was extended while various design options were considered and weapon systems evaluated and ordered. Consequently it was not until 1995 that the first ship (King Kwanggaeto) was laid down, and a further pair (Euljimundok and Yangmanchun) were started in 1996. However, the subsequent time taken to build and complete these ships was commendably short by international standards and they were completed in July 1998, and March and December 1999.

The final design bears more than a passing resemblance to the MEKO 200 frigates and a similar CODOG machinery installation has been used. An international armament outfit includes US-supplied Harpoon and Sea Sparrow missiles, an Italian 5in (127mm) gun, Dutch CIWS and a British-supplied Westland Lynx helicopter. Electronic equipment, including sonars, is sourced from America, The Netherlands, Britain and Germany. With propulsion machinery from America and Germany, these ships clearly illustrate the international and co-operative nature of many contemporary naval construction programmes.

To follow on from these ships, South Korea is planning to build up to six KDX-2 destroyers. These will be of similar appearance but the hull will be lengthened by approximately 60ft (18m) and full load displacement will rise to 4,800 tons. This will allow the air defence armament to be upgraded to Standard

SM-2R missiles housed in a Mk.41 VLS silo on the lengthened foredeck, while Mk.31 RAM missiles will supplement the close-in defence. An initial order for three ships was approved in 1998 with the first to be laid down in 2001 for completion in 2004.

SPECIFICATION

Type: DDG
Class: Okpo
Displacement: 3,855 tons full load
Length: 444.2ft (135.4m)
Beam: 46.6ft (14.2m)
Draught: 13.8ft (4.2m)
Machinery: CODOG; 2 LM2500 gas turbines, 58,200hp; 2 MTU 20V 956TB92 diesels, 8,000hp; 2 shafts
Speed & Range: 30kt; 4,000 miles (6,440km) at 18kt
Complement: 170
Missiles: 2 quadruple fixed launchers, Boeing Harpoon long-range SSM; Mk.48 16-cell VLS, Sea Sparrow short-range SAM
Guns: 1 Otobreda 5in (127mm)/54 automatic; 2 Goalkeeper 7-barrelled 30mm CIWS
ASW & USW: 2 triple Mk.32 324mm (12.75in) torpedo tubes, Mk.46 A/S torpedoes; SLQ-25 Nixie towed decoy
Sensors: radar: SP-49(V)5 air search; MW08 surface search; STIR 180 fire control; SPS55M navigation
Aircraft: 1 helicopter

INDIA
FFG, Godavari

THE BOXED DATA APPLY TO three Modified Godavari class frigates (*Bramaputra*, *Beas*, *Betwa*) which are due to commission between 2000 and 2004, although they differ from the three Godavaris (*Godavari*, *Gomati*, *Ganga*), which were completed in the mid-1980s mainly in terms of an improved armament outfit including the SS-N-25 anti-ship missiles and the Trishul SAM for air defence.

The Godavari design is based upon the very successful British Leander class frigate introduced in the 1960s, four of these having been built in India between 1967 and 1981 as the Nilgiri class. However, the Indian adaptation of the classic Leander design has changed the outline of the ships beyond recognition. Although employing a similar, but lengthened, hull and the same steam machinery plant, the superstructure is heavily built up with the hangar extending to the full beam. A much heavier armament, mostly of Russian origin, is carried and comprises a twin 57mm (2.2in) gun forward, four fixed launchers for SS-N-2D Styx SSMs, a twin launcher for SS-N-4 Gecko short-range SAMs, four twin 30mm gun mountings around the superstructure and two triple 324mm (12.75in) A/S torpedo tubes. Full load displacement has risen by some 900 tons and the larger hangar allows two Sea King helicopters to be embarked, compared to a single Lynx on Royal Navy Leanders.

Of the three Modified Godavari class frigates, only one has been completed, and although the other two were laid down in 1994 and 1996, their construction has been considerably delayed and they are yet to enter service.

Gomati *(F21), one of three Godavari class frigates built in India and based on a much modified Leander class design. (Guy Toremans)*

SPECIFICATION

Type: FFG
Class: Godavari
Displacement: 3,850 tons full load
Length: 414.9ft (126.5m)
Beam: 47.6ft (14.5m)
Draught: hull 14.8ft (4.5m)
Machinery: 2 boilers, 2 Bhopal turbines, 30,000hp; 2 shafts
Speed & Range: 27kt; 4,500 miles (7,240km) at 12kt
Complement: 313
Missiles: 4 quadruple fixed launchers, SS-N-25 (KH-35 Uran) long-range SSM; Trishul short-range SAM
Guns: 1 OTO Melera 3in (76mm\)/62 automatic gun; 4 AK630 6-barrelled 30mm CIWS
ASW & USW: 2 triple ILAS3 torpedo tubes, A244S A/S torpedoes
Sensors: radar: Signaal LW08 long-range air search; Head Net C air and surface search; I-band navigation; Seaguard, Aparna and Bass Tilt fire control; sonar: APSOH hull-mounted medium-frequency active search and attack; VDS
Aircraft: 2 helicopters

FRANCE
FFG, La Fayette

Surcouf *(F711), La Fayette* class frigate.
(Marine Nationale, France)

THESE STRIKING-LOOKING FRIGATES are among the first generation of so-called stealth ships whose design is optimised to reduce their detectability by radar and other sensors. The clean lines with angled surfaces cause the minimum of energy to be reflected back to the illuminating source, and this type of outline will become increasingly common in the future.

The first of this class, FNS *La Fayette*, was laid down in December 1990 and commissioned on 23 March 1996. Three more ships *(Surcouf, Courbet, Aconit)* are currently in service and a fifth *(Guépratte)* is due for completion in January 2002. Unusually for a modern frigate, these ships have no anti-submarine capability at all and are optimised for the surface warfare role with Exocet missiles and a medium-calibre gun. The Crotale surface-to-air missile is basically for self-defence purposes while the single Aérospatiale AS 565MA Panther helicopter carries no offensive armament other than a pair of machine-guns, its main use being to locate over-the-horizon targets for the ship's Exocet missiles. The hangar and flightdeck is capable of accommodating larger helicopters such as the NFH-90.

Most of these ships are deployed to the Pacific and Indian oceans where they provide maritime support for French possessions in the area and where their lack of ASW capability is not significant. However, a projected anti-submarine version may be built, and the basic design has won some export success with three ordered by Saudi Arabia and another six by Taiwan. The Saudi vessels will be armed with four fixed 21in (533mm) torpedo tubes for A/S homing torpedoes and Aster 15 medium-range SAMs using VLS silos set into the foredeck, as well as the Exocet missiles and 3.9in (100mm) gun which feature in the original French version. In addition, the Singapore Navy has recently ordered six new 3,000-ton stealth frigates to be built in France utilising experience gained with the La Fayette class.

Courbet *(F712), demonstrating the clean stealth profile of these ships.
(Marine Nationale, France)

SPECIFICATION

Type: FFG
Class: La Fayette
Displacement: 3,700 tons full load
Length: 407.5ft (124.2m)
Beam: 50.5ft (15.4m)
Draught: 19.4ft (5.9m)
Machinery: CODAD; 4 SEMT-Pielstick 12 PA6 V280STC diesels, 21,100hp; 2 shafts, cp propellers; bow thruster
Speed & Range: 25kt; 9,000 miles (14,480km) at 12kt
Complement: 163
Missiles: 2 quadruple launchers, MM38 Exocet SSM; 1 octuple launcher, Crotale short-range SAM
Guns: 1 DCN 3.9in (100mm)/55 automatic gun; 2 Giat G20F 20mm guns; 2 12.7mm (0.5in) machine-guns
ASW & USW: nil
Sensors: radar: Thompson CSF Sea Tiger DRBV 15C air and surface search; Racal Decca 1229 (DRBN 34A) navigation; Thompson CSF Castor 2J fire control
Aircraft: 1 helicopter

FF, ANZAC

Above and right: Arunta *(151), the second of eight ANZAC class frigates for the RAN. (CelsiusTech)*

THE ANZAC CLASS IS A JOINT Australian and New Zealand programme, although all ships are being built in Australia. Eight have been ordered for the RAN with the first three (*Anzac, Arunta, Warramunga*) in service by 2001 and the remainder due to be completed by the end of 2004. The original contract, awarded to the specially formed Australian Marine Engineering Consolidated in November 1989, was for eight Australian ships and two more for the Royal New Zealand Navy.

The design was based on the very successful Blohm und Voss MEKO 200 frigate which had already been adopted by several other navies including those of Turkey and Portugal. As completed, the Australian ships are armed only with a 5in (127mm) gun, and a basic eight-cell VLS Sea Sparrow self-defence missile system, as well as A/S torpedoes. This is a relatively light armament outfit for ships of this size, and a warfighting improvement programme (WIP) was planned to increase their capability in defence against anti-ship missiles and in the AAW role by the addition of a VLS for medium-range SAMs. Such improvements might have involved a lengthening of the hull and would have been very expensive. Consequently, the WIP project was cancelled in late 1999 and efforts will be concentrated on improving defences against anti-ship missiles. However, the planned modernisation to fit Harpoon SSMs will go ahead, as will the introduction of Evolved Sea Sparrow SAMs.

The initial New Zealand order was for two ships (*Te Kaha* and *Te Mana*), which commissioned in 1997 and 1999, with options on a further two ships, although these will now not be built. The RNZN ships will not be equipped with Harpoon. Both countries will operate a single SH-2G Seasprite multi-role helicopter from each of these frigates but, pending delivery of definitive aircraft, the RAN will use existing Sikorsky SH-60B Seahawks while the RNZN has taken delivery of four ex-USN SH-2Fs.

SPECIFICATION

Type: FF
Class: ANZAC
Displacement: 3,600 tons full load
Length: 387.1ft (118m)
Beam: 48.6ft (14.8m)
Draught: 14.3ft (4.35m)
Machinery: CODOG; 2 LM 2500 gas turbines, 30,172hp; 2 MTU 12V 1163 TB83 diesels, 8,840hp; 2 shafts, cp propellers
Speed & Range: 27kt; 6,000 miles (9,650km) at 18kt
Complement: 163
Missiles: 2 quadruple launchers, Boeing Harpoon SSM (planned); Mk.41 octuple VLS silo, Sea Sparrow short-range SAM
Guns: 1 5in (127mm)/54 or 62 Mk.45 automatic gun
ASW & USW: 2 Mk.32 triple 324mm (12.75in) torpedo tubes, Mk.46 A/S torpedoes; SLQ-25A towed decoy
Sensors: radar: SPS-49(V)8 long-range air search; Celsius Tech 9LV 453 TIR combined air/surface search and fire control; Atlas 9600 ARPA navigation; sonar: Spherion B Mod. 5 hull-mounted medium-frequency search and attack; Passive towed array projected
Aircraft: 1 helicopter

FFG, Bremen (Type 122)

THE BREMEN DESIGN IS ADAPTED FROM the Dutch Kortenaer class, from which it differs mainly in having a CODOG propulsion system instead of an all-gas-turbine outfit. In the 1970s considerable effort was put into trying to achieve a Standard NATO frigate design with Germany, The Netherlands and the United Kingdom all having major construction programmes. However, as with many collaborative naval programmes, the participants could not agree on a common specification and went their own way.

In the case of the German Navy, US pressure to fit General Electric LM2500 gas turbines instead of the British Olympus powerplants resulted in a higher fuel consumption. In order to counteract this, it was decided to fit MTU diesels as the cruise machinery so that a CODOG system replaced the original COGOG and the internal structure of the ship had to be considerably altered. The German SATIR action information system was installed and the hangar enlarged to the full width of the ship so that two SH-60 LAMPS III helicopters could be carried. In the event they proved too large and the German Navy also adopted the Westland Lynx Mk.88.

As a result of these changes the construction programme lagged behind the Dutch, and the first F122 (Bremen) was not laid down until July 1979 and was completed in May 1982. The other six ships were Niedersachsen (completed 1982), Rheinland-Pfalz (1983), Emden (1983), Köln (1984), Karlsruhe (1984), Augsburg (1989) and Lübeck (1990). The construction programme was unusual in that the hulls were built and fitted with some machinery at one of five shipyards and, after launching, were towed to Bremer Vulkan (Bremen) for completion and the installation of electronics and weapons systems. A modular construction technique was used which led to some remarkably quick times between laying down the first section on the slipway and the subsequent launching – less than six months in some cases.

Since entering service the Bremen class frigates have been improved by the addition of twin RAM launchers on the hangar roof to supplement the Sea Sparrow missiles at short range, and the Signaal DA08 long-range radar is being replaced by the DASA TRS-3D/32, which offers better target discrimination capability.

Bremen (F207), Type 122 frigate. (German Navy)

Lübeck (F214), the last of eight Type 122 frigates. (German Navy)

SPECIFICATION

Type: FFG
Class: Bremen (Type 122)
Displacement: 3,680 tons full load
Length: 426.4 ft (130m)
Beam: 47.6ft (14.5m)
Draught: 21.3ft (6.6m)
Machinery: CODOG, 2 GE LM2500 gas turbines, 51,000hp; 2 MTU 20V 956 TB92 diesels, 11,070hp; 2 shafts, cp propellers
Speed & Range: 30kt (20kt diesel); 4,000 miles (6,440km) at 18kt
Complement: 219
Missiles: 2 quadruple launchers, Boeing Harpoon long-range SSM; 1 Mk.29 octuple launcher, Sea Sparrow short-range SAM; 2 21-cell launchers, RAM short range SAM
Guns: 1 OTO Melera 3in (76mm) automatic gun; 2 single 20mm or 27mm guns
ASW & USW: 2 twin 324mm (12.75in) fixed torpedo tubes, Mk.46 A/S torpedoes
Sensors: radar: Signaal DA08 air and surface search; SMA3 RM20 navigation; Signaal STIR and WM25 fire control; sonar: Atlas DSQS-21BZ medium-frequency active search and attack
Aircraft: 2 helicopters

FFG, Krivak (Type 1135)

THIS VERY LARGE CLASS of anti-submarine escorts was in continuous production from 1968 until 1990. Some 39 were built in three distinct subgroups and the original Krivak I was the world's first major class of warship to be powered entirely by gas turbines, the uptakes venting through a single squat funnel set well aft. The Krivak I disposed the missile armament mostly forward, quadruple torpedo tubes amidships and two twin 3in (76mm) gun mountings right aft. This arrangement was repeated in the Krivak II, but the gun armament was altered to two single 3.9in (100mm) guns.

Neither of these versions had any provision for operating a helicopter, but the Krivak III, of which eight were completed between 1983 and 1993, incorporated some substantial changes including the provision of a hangar and flightdeck on the stern. A single Kamov Ka-27 Helix is carried. This alteration necessitated the deletion of the after SA-N-4 launcher and also the two gun mountings. Instead, a single 3.9in (100mm) automatic was mounted on the foredeck in place of the quadruple launcher for the SS-N-14 ASW missiles, which were no longer carried. Interestingly, the Krivak IIIs were not originally built for the Soviet Navy but for the USSR Border Guard, which was run by the KGB. However, all are now in regular naval service with the exception of the last to be completed, which was ceded to the Ukraine after the break-up of the Soviet Union.

In 1997 India ordered six frigates based on the Krivak III hull and machinery, but armament and equipment installation is yet to be decided and may well differ from that of the Russian ships. The first ship of this order is being built at St Petersburg and is due for completion in 2002.

A total of 20 Krivak Is were completed between 1970 and 1982, and these were followed by 11 Krivak IIs, which commissioned between 1975 and 1982. Many of these two groups have been retired and three ships were transferred to the Ukraine Navy in 1997, although none appear to be currently operational.

Ladny*, a Krivak I class (Type 1135) anti-submarine frigate.*
(RAF Kinloss/MoD)

SPECIFICATION

Type: FFG
Class: Krivak (Type 1135)
Displacement: 3,100 tons standard, 3,650 tons full load
Length: 405.2ft (123.5m)
Beam: 46.9ft (14.3m)
Draught: 16.4ft (5m)
Machinery: COGAG; 2 M8K gas turbines, 55,500hp; 2 M62 gas turbines, 13,600hp; 2 shafts
Speed & Range: 32kt; 4,000 miles (6,440km) at 14kt
Complement: 194
Missiles: 2 quadruple fixed launchers, SS-N-25 SSM; 1 quadruple launcher, SS-N-14 Silex SSM or A/S torpedo-carrying missile; 2 twin launchers, SA-N-4 Gecko SAM
Guns: 2 twin 3in (76mm) or 2 single 3.9in (100mm) automatic guns; 2 AK630 30mm CIWS (Krivak III only)
ASW & USW: 2 quadruple 21in (533mm) torpedo tubes, various torpedoes; 2 RBU 6000 12-barrelled A/S mortar
Sensors: radar: Head Net or Top Plate long-range air search; Don Kay, Palm Frond, Don 2 or Spin Trough surface search; various fire control including Eye Bowl, Pop Group, Owl Screech, Kite Screech and Bass Tilt; sonar: Bull Nose hull-mounted medium-frequency search and attack; Mare Tail or Steer Hide medium-frequency active VDS
Aircraft: 1 helicopter (Krivak III only)

Krivak class (Type 1135) anti-submarine frigate.
(RAF Kinloss/MoD)

FFG, Kortenaer/van Heemskerck

Witte de Withe (F813), air defence version of the Kortenaer class frigate.
(Rolls-Royce)

installation of the Mk.13 launcher system for the Standard SM-1MR long-range surface-to-air missile, together with one of two Signaal STIR240 target-tracking radars (the other is mounted atop the bridge superstructure). The 3in (76mm) OTO Melera gun on the foredeck is also deleted to make room for the Mk.29 octuple launcher for Sea Sparrow short-range SAMs. Finally, a Goalkeeper CIWS is mounted right aft on the stern. Both of these ships, and the two remaining standard Kortenaers, are fitted with twin SATCOM antennae, carried on high platforms just forward of the funnel.

THIS VERY SUCCESSFUL CLASS OF TEN general-purpose frigates was completed between 1978 and 1983. These ships were contemporary with the British Type 22 frigates and, although efforts to achieve common design did not come to fruition, both classes used the same Olympus/Tyne gas turbine machinery installation and each had a twin hangar to allow operation of two Westland SH-14 Lynx helicopters. In addition, the Dutch design formed the basis of the German F122 class frigates.

As completed, the first two Kortenaers had a second 3in (76mm) gun on the hangar roof but this was later replaced by a single 40mm gun as in the rest of the class, although all eventually received the Goalkeeper 30mm CIWS. Of the 10 standard ships built, two were sold to Greece while under construction while a further four were subsequently transferred to the Hellenic Navy between 1993 and 1997 as they were replaced in Dutch service by the new M class frigates. Another two were sold to the United Arab Emirates and two more were retired in 1999/2000, leaving only two currently operational with the *Koninklijke Marine*. These will both be retired by the end of 2001.

Two air defence versions of the basic Kortenaer design, known as the Jacob van Heemskerck class, were commissioned in 1986 and these will remain in service until at least 2004/5 when they will eventually be replaced by two of the new DDGs currently on order. The van Heemskerck class frigates differ substantially from the standard Kortenaers in that the hangar and helicopter flightdeck have been deleted in order to allow the

SPECIFICATION

Type: FFG
Class: Kortenaer
Displacement: 3,050 tons standard, 3,630 tons full load
Length: 428ft (130.5m)
Beam: 47.9ft (14.6m)
Draught: 14.1ft (4.3m)
Machinery: COGOG; 2 Rolls-Royce TM3B gas turbines, 50,880hp; 2 Rolls-Royce Tyne RM1C gas turbines, 9,900hp; 2 shafts, cp propellers
Speed & Range: 30kt; 4,700 miles (7,560km) at 16kt
Complement: 176 (200 max.)
Missiles: 2 quadruple launchers, Boeing Harpoon SSM; 1 Mk.29 octuple launcher, Sea Sparrow short-range SAM
Guns: 1 3in (76mm)/62 OTO Melera compact Mk.100 automatic gun; 1 30mm Goalkeeper CIWS
ASW & USW: 2 twin 324mm (12.75in) torpedo tubes, Mk.46 A/S torpedoes
Sensors: radar: Signaal LW08 long-range air search; Signaal SW06 surface search; Signaal STIR and WM25 fire control; sonar: Westinghouse SQS-509 medium-frequency active search and attack
Aircraft: 1 helicopter

DENMARK
FF, Thetis

Vaedderen *(F359)*, the third Thetis class patrol frigate off Cape Town Bay. *(CelsiusTech)*

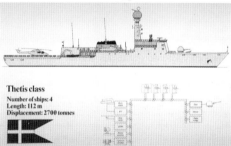

Thetis class
Number of ships: 4
Length: 112 m
Displacement: 2700 tonnes

Drawing of Thetis class frigate. *(CelsiusTech)*

THE EXTENSION OF NATIONAL RIGHTS in the form of economic zones stretching out to 200 miles (320km) offshore has given rise to a requirement to patrol and police such areas. The use of conventional warships for such purposes is expensive and consequently many navies have introduced vessels specifically designed for this role. The Danish Thetis class is an excellent example of this trend, carrying a modest armament in a roomy and seaworthy hull which is capable of extended patrols. It should not be forgotten that Denmark also has sovereignty over the Faeroe Isles and Greenland, and therefore has vast areas of inhospitable waters to cover. Consequently, these ships have strengthened hulls to enable them to operate in the Arctic. For the same reason, an enclosed lookout position is built into the top of the plated mast structure, immediately below the radome containing the Plessey/Siemens AWS-6 radar.

Despite their size, these vessels are lightly armed, although there are plans to fit a suitable surface-to-air missile system such as Sea Sparrow for self-defence. In addition, the design allows for the installation of modularised weapons systems as utilised in the Danish Standardflex ships. A single Westland Lynx Mk.91 is operated from the spacious flightdeck on the stern which can, if required, accommodate the much larger Sea King or EHI Merlin helicopter.

A total of four Thetis class ships were ordered in 1987. The name ship was laid down in the following year and completed in 1991. She was followed by *Triton* (1991), *Vaedderen* (1992) and *Hvidbjørnen* (1992), and these replaced the four ships of the original Hvidbjørnen class which had been completed in 1963 and were retired as the new ships entered service.

SPECIFICATION

Type: FF
Class: Thetis
Displacement: 2,600 tons standard, 3,500 tons full load
Length: 369.1ft (112.5m)
Beam: 47.2ft (14.4m)
Draught: 19.7ft (6m)
Machinery: 3 MAN/B&W Alpha 12V 28/32A diesels, 10,800hp; 1 shaft, cp propeller; bow and azimuth thrusters
Speed & Range: 20kt; 8,500 miles (13,680km) at 15kt
Complement: 72 (max.)
Missiles: SAM planned
Guns: 1 OTO Melera 3in (76mm)/62 automatic; 2 Oerlikon 20mm
ASW & USW: depth charges
Sensors: radar: Plessey AWS 6 air and surface search; Terma Scanter Mil surface search; FR1505DA navigation; Bofors 9LV Mk.3 fire control
Aircraft: 1 helicopter

FFG, Karel Doorman (M Class)

HESE EIGHT M CLASS FRIGATES were all built by Koninklijke Maatschappij De Schelde (Flushing) and were nominally intended to replace the older Van Speijk class frigates, a Dutch version of the British Leander class. However, they are much more capable ships, being almost equivalent to the slightly larger Kortenaer class frigates which are now also supplanting, and present a handsome appearance with a flush deck and neat superstructure blocks.

Although not obviously stealthy like many later designs, considerable efforts have been made to reduce the radar and infra-red signatures. An unusual feature is the positioning of the 16 VLS cells for the Evolved Sea Sparrow missile system in a row of eight pairs along the port side of the hangar. The hangar itself, and the large flightdeck on the stern, are sized to accommodate the forthcoming NH-90 multi-role helicopter, but all ships currently carry a single Westland SH-14 Lynx equipped with a search radar and dipping sonar, and can carry two Mk.46 torpedoes.

Since the first ships entered service, improvements made include an upgraded action data system and command system, the addition of a towed array sonar, and the installation of a SATCOM system. The antennae for this latter system are carried in two prominent spherical domes either side of the mainmast. Apart from this, and the Racal navigation radar, virtually all the radar and other electronic equipment is of Dutch manufacture.

The lead ship (*Karel Doorman*) was laid down in February 1985, launched on 20 April 1988 and commissioned on 31 May 1991. The remaining seven ships were laid down between November 1985 and October 1991. Names and completion dates were: *Willem van der Zaan* (1991), *Tjerk Hiddes* (1992), *Van Amstel* (1993), *Abraham van der Hulst* (1993), *Van Nes* (1994), *Van Galen* (1994) and *Van Speijk* (1995).

HNLMS **Abraham van der Hulst** *(F832),*
***Karel Doorman** class frigate.*
(author)

SPECIFICATION

Type: FFG
Class: Karel Doorman (M Class)
Displacement: 3,320 tons full load
Length: oa 401.2ft (122.3m), wl 374.7ft (114.2m)
Beam: 47.2ft (14.4m)
Draught: 14.1ft (4.3m)
Machinery: CODOG; 2 Rolls-Royce Spey SM1C gas turbines, 33,800hp; 2 Stork-Wartsilä 12SW280 diesels, 9,790hp; 2 shafts, cp propellers
Speed & Range: 30kt (21kt diesels); 5,000 miles (8,050km) at 18kt
Complement: 156 (163 max.)
Missiles: 2 quadruple launchers, Boeing Harpoon SSM; 16 Mk.48 VLS launchers, Sea Sparrow short-range SAM
Guns: 1 3in (76mm)/62 OTO Melera compact Mk.100 automatic gun; 1 30mm Goalkeeper CIWS
ASW & USW: 2 twin 324mm (12.75in) torpedo tubes, Mk.46 A/S torpedoes; SLQ-25 towed torpedo decoy
Sensors: radar: Signaal LW08 long-range air search; Signaal SMART 3D air and surface search; Racal Decca 1226 navigation; Signaal STIR fire control; sonar: Signaal PHS-36 medium-frequency active search and attack; DSBV-61 passive towed array
Aircraft: 1 helicopter

DDG, MEKO 360

THE MEKO 360 WAS THE FIRST of the Blohm und Voss modular frigate designs to achieve export success with a single order placed by Nigeria in 1977. This was subsequently followed by a more substantial order from Argentina for six ships, placed in 1978. Four of these were actually completed (*Almirante Brown*, *La Argentina*, *Heroina*, *Sarandi*) and commissioned in 1983 and 1984, although the remaining pair was cancelled in favour of the smaller MEKO 140.

One of the benefits of the MEKO concept was that the customer could choose a range of equipment options within the basic hull, and consequently the Argentine Navy chose the Olympus/Tyne COGOG machinery installation in order to maintain commonality with its two existing Type 42 destroyers. In fact, the two ships make an interesting comparison as they are of a very similar displacement and overall dimensions, but the MEKO design has a more balanced armament, particularly in terms of the close-range defences which the British ships sorely lacked at the time of the Falklands War. Initially, the Argentine ships embarked an Alouette III torpedo-carrying helicopter, but in 1996 these were replaced by the AS 555C Fennec. The four MEKO 360s are the most powerful surface ships in the Argentine fleet, and one, *Almirante Brown*, was deployed to the Persian Gulf in 1990/91 as part of the UN forces engaged against Iraq.

In contrast, the career of the single Nigerian vessel (*Aradu*) has been less successful, and it has been involved in several accidents and groundings and has spent much time laid up under repair. She differed from the Argentine ships mainly in having a CODOG propulsion system with Olympus gas turbines and MTU diesels. The armament outfit was similar and a single Lynx Mk.89 was embarked.

Sarandi (D13), one of four MEKO 360s designated as destroyers by the Argentine Navy. (Blohm und Voss GmbH)

Aradu (F89), the single MEKO 360 built for the Nigerian Navy. (Blohm und Voss GmbH)

SPECIFICATION

Type: DDG
Class: MEKO 360
Displacement: 2,900 tons standard, 3,360 tons full load
Length: 412.1ft (125.6m)
Beam: 43.1ft (15.0m)
Draught: 14.1ft (4.3m)
Machinery: COGOG; 2 Rolls-Royce TM3B Olympus gas turbines, 50,000hp; 2 Rolls-Royce RM1C Tyne gas turbines, 10,000hp; 2 shafts, cp propellers
Speed & Range: 30kt; 5,180 miles (8,330km) at 18kt
Complement: 200
Missiles: 2 fixed quadruple launchers, MM40 Exocet SSM; 1 octuple Albatros launcher, Aspide medium-range SAM
Guns: 1 OTO Melera 5in (127mm)/54 automatic; 4 Breda/Bofors twin 40mm/70; 2 single Oerlikon 20mm guns
ASW & USW: 2 ILAS 3 triple 324mm (12.75in) torpedo tubes, A244 A/S torpedoes; Graseby G1738 towed torpedo decoy
Sensors: radar: Signaal DB08A air and surface search; Signaal ZW06 surface search; STIR and WM25 fire control; Decca 1226 navigation; sonar: DSQS-21BZ hull-mounted medium-frequency search and attack
Aircraft: 1 helicopter

FFG, MEKO 200

Yavuz (F240), a MEKO 200 of the Turkish Navy. (Blohm und Voss GmbH)

Barboros (F244), Modified MEKO 200, Turkish Navy. (Blohm und Voss GmbH)

THE MEKO 200 IS AN EXTREMELY successful design which has gained substantial export orders for the German shipbuilding industry. In each case the hull and general outline of the ship is identical but customers can choose a variety of armament and machinery combinations which are installed on a modular basis.

Greece made a formal decision to order four MEKO 200 frigates in 1988, and the first of class (Hydra) was ordered in February 1989. Built by Blohm und Voss at Hamburg, it was completed in November 1992. Three further ships were laid down at Hellenic shipyards, Skaramanga, and the first of these commissioned in April 1996, and the last pair in 1998. The boxed data refer to these ships, which carry a single Sikorsky SH-70B-6 Aegean Hawk helicopter.

Prior to the Greek order, Portugal had also ordered three MEKO 200s in 1986, and these were all laid down in 1989. Built in Germany by Blohm und Voss and Howaldtswerke, they were completed in 1991 and are basically very similar to the Greek ships with the same hull, machinery and some of the weapons systems. The principal difference lies in the main armament where a French-built 3.9in (100mm) gun replaces the FMC 5in (127mm)/54, and the Sea Sparrows are fired from an octuple Mk.29 launcher instead of a VLS. The hangar and flightdeck are optimised for two Super Lynx Mk.95 helicopters.

The earliest customer for the MEKO 200, however, was Turkey, which ordered four Yavuz class ships in 1982, two of which were built in Germany and two in Turkey. They were very similar to the Greek ships described above but had a Mk.29 octuple

launcher for the Sea Sparrows on the hangar roof and also carried three Oerlikon-Contraves Sea Zenith 25mm CIWS. This is an unusual weapon system which can elevate through 90° in order to engage targets vertically above the ship. Each four-barrelled mounting can fire 3,400 rounds per minute. Turkey subsequently ordered four more MEKO 200s to a slightly modified design in 1990, and again two were built in Germany and two in Turkey. Known as the Barbaros class, they differed from their predecessors in that they were slightly larger and utilised the popular CODOG machinery installation instead of an all-diesel system. Some ships also incorporated a Mk.41 VLS for Aspide medium-range SAMs.

Other customers for the MEKO 200 include Australia and New Zealand, whose Anzac class frigates are described separately.

SPECIFICATION

Type: FFG
Class: MEKO 200
Displacement: 2,710 tons, 3,350 tons full load
Length: 383.9ft (117m)
Beam: 48.6ft (14.8m)
Draught: 19.7ft (6m)
Machinery: CODOG; 2 LM2500 gas turbines, 60,000hp; 2 MTU 20V 956 TB82 diesels, 10,420hp; 2 shafts, cp propellers
Speed & Range: 31kt; 4,100 miles (6,600km) at 15kt
Complement: 173
Missiles: 2 fixed quadruple launchers, Boeing Harpoon long-range SSM; 16-cell Mk.48 VLS, Sea Sparrow short-range SAM
Guns: 1 FMC 5in (127mm)/54 automatic; 2 Vulcan/Phalanx 6-barrelled 20mm CIWS
ASW & USW: 2 Mk.32 triple 324mm (12.75in) torpedo tubes, Mk.46 A/S torpedoes; SLQ-25 Nixie torpedo decoy
Sensors: radar: Signaal MW08 air search; DA08 air and surface search; Racal Decca 2690BT navigation; STIR fire control; sonar: SQS-56/DE 1160 combined hull-mounted and VDS
Aircraft: 1 helicopter

UNITED STATES
FFG, Oliver Hazard Perry

USS Jarrett (FFG-33), Oliver Hazard Perry class frigate. (US Navy)

THIS LARGE CLASS OF FRIGATES was originally designed as second line escorts but the retirement of older frigates and destroyers led to them being adapted for a variety of roles, and the full load displacement is now some 500 tons greater than originally envisaged. In all, some 51 ships were built for the US Navy and it has proved popular with other navies. Four were built in Seattle for the Australian Navy, which also ordered two more from Australian yards. A further six were built in Spain, and Taiwan constructed seven. In addition, some US ships were transferred to other navies, including six to Turkey, four to Egypt and one each to Bahrain and Poland.

The US construction programme spanned some 14 years with the lead ship being laid down in December 1975 and the last, USS *Ingraham*, commissioning in August 1989. Currently there are approximately 35 of these ships active with the US Navy.

The original design was produced to a fixed budget, which resulted in some significant operational limitations, particularly with the ships' ability to absorb battle damage, as was shown by incidents in the Persian Gulf involving the *Stark* (FFG-31) and *Samuel B. Roberts* (FFG-58). Nevertheless, some 14 ships of the class were deployed to the Gulf area during the 1991 war, illustrating the importance of these frigates to US naval operations.

The profile of the Perry class is unusual with a large superstructure surmounted by a squat funnel aft and the single 3in (76mm) gun amidships. The single Mk.13 launcher on the foredeck can handle either Harpoon SSMs or Standard SM-1MR SAMs, with magazine capacity for four of the former and 36 of the latter. The original design featured a single hangar, but this has been modified to provide twin hangars housing two SH-60B Seahawk or SH-2G Seasprite helicopters.

SPECIFICATION

Type: FFG
Class: Oliver Hazard Perry
Displacement: 2,750 tons standard, up to 4,100 tons full load
Length: 445ft (135.6m)
Beam: 45ft (13.7m)
Draught: hull 14.8ft (4.5m)
Machinery: 2 GE LM2500 gas turbines, 41,000hp; 1 shaft, cp propeller; 2 auxiliary retractable propellers, 650hp
Speed & Range: 29kt; 4,500 miles (7,240km) at 20kt
Complement: 200
Missiles: 1 Mk.13 Mod. 4 single launcher system for Boeing Harpoon long-range SSM and Standard SM-1MR SAM
Guns: 1 OTO Melera 3in (76mm)/62 Mk.75 automatic gun; 1 Vulcan/Phalanx 6-barrelled 20mm CIWS; 2 single 25mm (option) and 4 12.7mm (0.5in) machine guns
ASW & USW: 2 Mk.32 triple 324mm (12.75in) torpedo tubes, Mk.46 A/S torpedoes
Sensors: radar: SPS-49(V)4 or 5 air search; SPS-55 surface search; SPG-60/STIR fire control; navigation; sonar: SQQ 89(V)2 comprising SQS 56 hull-mounted active search and attack and SQR 19 passive towed array
Aircraft: 2 helicopters

FFG, Maestrale/Lupo

EIGHT OF THESE FAST AND POWERFUL general-purpose Maestrale class frigates were completed between 1982 and 1985. The design is based upon the preceding Lupo class, of which four were built in the late 1970s, the main difference being a 33ft (10m) increase in length which allowed a larger hangar and flightdeck so that an additional helicopter could be carried.

Although only four Lupo class frigates were built for the Italian Navy, the design scored several export successes, and four were built for Peru and another six for Venezuela. Iraq also ordered four, which were launched between 1983 and 1985, but delivery was suspended, initially because of payment difficulties, and then finally cancelled in 1990 following the UN embargo on arms sales to Iraq. These ships were eventually taken over by the Italian Navy and commissioned between 1994 and 1996 as the Artigliere class. They were built by Fincantieri at its Ancona and Riva Trigosa shipyards.

New weapons and communications systems were fitted to meet the requirements of the Italian Navy and the helicopter deck at the stern has a single landing spot for an Agusta Bell AB 212 helicopter. The larger Maestrale class frigates can carry two of these helicopters and, apart from their greater length, they can be distinguished by the fact that the Teseo SSM launchers are positioned on the hangar roof instead of abreast the funnel and superstructure as on the Lupo and Artigliere classes.

The Italian shipbuilding industry is one of the few world-wide which can supply all the elements of a modern warship including guns, missiles, electronics and machinery systems, and this accounts in part for the export successes achieved with these frigates.

Perseo (F566), Lupo class frigate.
(Marina Militare, Italy)

Grecale (F571), Maestrale class frigate.
(Marina Militare, Italy)

SPECIFICATION

Type: FFG
Class: Maestrale/Lupo
Displacement: 2,500 tons standard, 3,200 tons full load
Length: 405ft (122.7m)
Beam: 42.5ft (12.9m)
Draught: 15.1ft (4.6ft)
Machinery: CODOG; 2 LM2500 gas turbines, 50,000hp; 2 GMT BL230.20DVM diesels, 12,600hp; 2 shafts, cp propellers
Speed & Range: 32kt; 6,000 miles (9,650km) at 16kt
Complement: 232
Missiles: 4 single fixed launchers, OTO Melera Teseo long-range SSM; 1 Albatros octuple launcher, Aspide short-range SAM
Guns: 1 OTO Melera 3in (76mm)/54 automatic; 2 twin Breda 40mm /70 CIWS; 2 single 20mm or 25mm guns can be fitted if required
ASW & USW: 2 Mk.32 triple torpedo tubes, Mk.46 A/S torpedoes; SLQ-25 towed decoy; Prairie Masker noise suppression system
Sensors: radar: SPS-774 (RTN30X) air and surface search; SPS-702 surface search; SPN-703 navigation SPG-75 and 74 fire control; sonar: DE1164 combined hull-mounted and VDS search and attack
Aircraft: 2 AB 212ASW helicopters

FRANCE
FFG, Floreal

F IRST ORDERED IN 1989, the six ships of this class of ocean patrol vessels were completed between 1992 and 1994. They are all deployed to the Indian and Pacific oceans where France retains a number of small colonies. A single AS 565MA Panther helicopter is normally embarked, but the flightdeck can accept a larger AS 332F Super Puma for refuelling. In addition to the normal ship's complement, a detachment of 24 marines is also embarked, enabling the ship to put a landing party ashore to deal with typical colonial police actions if required. The four-diesel CODAD machinery allows great flexibility and economy of operation, resulting in a 10,000-mile (16,100 km) range at a typical cruising speed, a point of considerable relevance in the vastness of the Pacific. To reduce costs, these warships are built to mercantile marine standards, a common practice today for warships which are not intended for front-line combat. They are fully air conditioned and fitted with stabilisers.

In 1998 Morocco ordered two Floreal class frigates and both were laid down in 1999 for delivery in 20001/02.

From the point of view of habitability, endurance and range, these ships are a substantial improvement on the preceding D'Estienne d'Orves patrol frigates, of which 20 were completed between 1976 and 1984 (including three which eventually went to Argentina). On a full load displacement of 1,300 tons, they carried a single 3.9in (100mm) gun, fixed ASW torpedo tubes and Mistral short-range SAMs, as well as Exocet SSMs on some ships. Many of this class have been retired, and by 2002 only nine will remain in service.

Germinal (F735), the last of seven Floreal class frigates.
(Marine Nationale, France)

SPECIFICATION

Type: FFG
Class: Floreal
Displacement: 2,600 tons standard, 2,950 tons full load
Length: 306.8ft (93.5m)
Beam: 45.9ft (14m)
Draught: 14.1ft (4.3m)
Machinery: CODAD; 4 SEMT-Pielstick 6 PA6 L280 diesels, 8,820hp; 2 shafts, cp propellers; bow thruster
Speed & Range: 20kt; 10,000 miles (16,100km) at 15kt
Complement: 86
Missiles: 2 single fixed launchers, Exocet MM38 SSM; 1 or 2 Simbad twin launchers, Mistral short-range SAM (optional instead of 20mm guns)
Guns: 1 3.9in (100mm)/55 CADAM automatic; 2 single 20mm
ASW & USW: nil
Sensors: radar: DRBV 21A air and surface search; DRBN 34A navigation and helicopter control
Aircraft: 1 helicopter

FFG, Jiangwei (Type 053 H2G)

THESE ARE MODERN FRIGATES with a powerful surface armament including long-range C801/802 anti-ship missiles, but a relatively limited anti-submarine capability in the shape of RBU 1200 five-barrelled fixed mortars mounted on the forecastle. The boxed data refer to the first four ships, which comprised the Jiangwei I class and were completed between December 1991 and April 1994. A further five Jiangwei II frigates were built between 1996 and the end of 1999, and these featured an improved SAM system with a lighter missile launcher, while the after 37mm guns were mounted on the hangar roof instead of on either side to give improved fields of fire. It is possible that the machinery installation in the later ships may comprise four instead of two diesels, raising maximum speed to 28kt. Both types carry a Harbin Z-9A helicopter, a licence-built version of the Eurocopter Dauphin. It is expected that two Jiangwei II frigates will eventually be built for Pakistan.

Prior to the Jiangwei class, China built large numbers of the smaller 1,450-ton Jianghu Type 053 frigate, between 1974 and 1996. These were of relatively conventional design with an armament of two single or twin 3.9in (100mm) guns and two twin launchers for the C-201 medium-range anti-ship missile. Again, ASW capability was minimal. Four other Jianghu class frigates were built (Types II, III and IV), and these had an increased displacement, extended superstructure and the longer-ranged C-801 missile. The sole Type II featured a hangar and flightdeck aft. However, there is a limit as to what can be packed into a small hull, and further production was cancelled in favour of the Jiangwei class described above, which featured a 92ft (28m) increase in overall length.

Huainan (540). One of four Type 053 H2G Jiangwei I class frigates of the People's Liberation Army Navy. (US Department of Defense)

SPECIFICATION

Type: FFG

Class: Jiangwei (Type 053 H2G)

Displacement: 2,250 tons full load

Length: 366.5ft (111.7m)

Beam: 39.7ft (12.1m)

Draught: 15.7ft (4.8m)

Machinery: 2 Type 12E 390 diesels, 14,400hp; 2 shafts

Speed & Range: 25kt; 4,000 miles (6,440km) at 18kt

Complement: 170

Missiles: 2 fixed triple launchers, C-801 or C-802 medium-long-range SSM; 1 sextuple launcher, CSA-N-2 short-range SAM

Guns: 1 twin 3.9in (100mm)/63; 4 twin 37mm/56

ASW & USW: 2 5-barrelled RBU 1200 A/S mortars

Sensors: radar: Knife Rest air and surface search; Sun Visor, Fog Lamp, Rice Lamp fire control; Racal Decca 1290 and China Type 360 navigation; sonar: Echo Type 5 hull-mounted active search and attack

Aircraft: 1 helicopter

MALAYSIA (UK)
FFG, Lekiu

Lekiu (30), one of two Malaysian frigates built in Britain. (D. Hannaford)

THESE TWO FRIGATES, *Lekiu* and *Jebat*, were ordered in March 1992 in a deal valued at £400 million and were laid down at Yarrow Shipbuilders, Glasgow, in 1994. The original commissioning dates should have been in February and May 1996 but completion was considerably delayed by problems with the combat information and control system, and they were not handed over until October and November 1999.

Classified as light frigates, they were built to the GEC Naval Systems Frigate 2000 design and carry powerful armament for this size of ship. Of particular interest is the British Seawolf SAM system which proved very successful in the Falklands but has achieved very few export orders, this installation being a rare example. The flightdeck and hangar are intended to allow operation of a Westland Super Lynx helicopter, six of which have been ordered by the Malaysian Navy, but until these are delivered the ships will deploy a single Westland Wasp.

Nevertheless, these two ships are the largest and most powerful units of the Malaysian Navy and the design applies current thinking in stealth technology. The heart of the combat system is the Alenia Marconi NAUTIS II command and fire control system which is centred around eight multi-function consoles in the operations room. The ship's self-protection capability is enhanced by a comprehensive ESM outfit and SuperBarricade 12-barrelled chaff and infra-red decoy launchers mounted in the bridge wings.

SPECIFICATION

Type: FFG
Class: Lekiu
Displacement: 1,845 tons standard, 2,390 tons full load
Length: 346ft (105.5m)
Beam: 42ft (12.8m)
Draught: 11.8ft (3.6m)
Machinery: CODAD; 4 MTU 20V1163 TB93 diesels, 33,300hp; 2 shafts, cp propellers
Speed & Range: 28kt; 5,000 miles (8,050km) at 14kt
Complement: 152
Missiles: 4 quadruple fixed launchers, Exocet MM40 medium-range SSM; 16-cell VLS silo, Seawolf short-range SAM
Guns: 1 Bofors 57mm (2.2in)/70 SAK Mk.2 automatic gun; 2 DS30B single 30mm guns
ASW & USW: 2 triple 324mm (12.75in) torpedo tubes, A/S torpedoes; Sea Siren torpedo decoy
Sensors: radar: Signaal DA08 air search; Ericsson Sea Giraffe surface search; Racal Decca navigation; Marconi 1802 fire control
Aircraft: 1 helicopter

SMALL WARSHIPS

NCLUDED IN THIS SECTION are descriptions of a selection of warships displacing 2,000 tons or less and these include missile-armed corvettes and fast attack craft, as well as a number of mine warfare vessels.

Even in World War II, the clearing of mines was a difficult affair as new influence mines, some dropped from aircraft, were introduced to supplement the traditional moored mine. With modern technology, mines have become increasingly complex and sophisticated and the measures needed to counteract them have become correspondingly more specialised. Although possessing the world's most powerful navy, the United States accorded a low priority to mine countermeasures during the Cold War years and suffered the consequences in the Gulf War when several of its ships were seriously damaged by mines. Fortunately, the European navies, used to operating in shallow waters and the littoral environment, had forged ahead in this area and have developed a sophisticated capability. Although some mine countermeasures vessels (MCMV) are equipped to sweep moored mines, most are also equipped with precision sonars to detect and locate seabed influence mines which are then dealt with by remotely operated undersea vehicles, or even attacked by dedicated mine destruction weapons such as the BAE Archerfish.

Any vessel equipped to deal with every type of mine would be large and expensive, so the concept of the single role minehunter (SRMH) has evolved in which the traditional minesweeping gear is not fitted. Some navies have gone a stage further and evolved a system of mine clearance using a flotilla of remotely controlled unmanned surface vessels controlled from a mother ship. The Danish Standardflex and its SAVs (surface auxiliary vessels) are a prime example.

OMAN (UK)
FSG, Qahir

THE TWO QAHIR CLASS CORVETTES, *Qahir al Amwaj* and *Al Mua'zzar* were ordered from the British shipbuilders Vosper Thornycroft in 1992. Vospers has a long tradition of building well-armed small warships for export and this design is no exception.

Laid down in 1993 and 1994, the two ships commissioned in September 1996 and April 1997. They present a balanced profile with gun and surface-to-surface missiles mounted on the foredeck and the Crotale SAM system aft of the squat funnel. Although a helicopter is not permanently embarked, the stern flightdeck is sized to accommodate a Super Puma-sized helicopter for refuelling and re-arming. Anti-submarine capability is limited, although provision is made for towed array sonar and triple 324mm (12.75in) torpedo tubes.

The Qahir class is an adaptation of Vosper Thornycroft's standard Vigilance design and incorporates many stealth features such as flat angled superstructure plating coated with radar-absorbent material to reduce radar signature and carefully shrouded exhausts to cut down IR emissions. Although built in the United Kingdom, there is a very international list of equipment fitted, including the Italian 3in (76mm) gun, French missile systems, Dutch radars as well as other British arms and electronics.

The Omani Navy also operates four Dhofar class missile-armed fast attack craft which were also built by Vosper Thornycroft and were completed in the 1980s. Armed with Exocet SAMs and a 3in (76mm) gun, these 300-ton vessels can make 38kt on four Paxman Valenta diesels producing 15,000hp.

Above and above right: Al Mua'zzar, *a 272ft (83m) corvette of the Omani Navy.* (Vosper Thornycroft)

SPECIFICATION

Type: FSG
Class: Qahir
Displacement: 1,450 tons full load
Length: 274.6ft (83.7m)
Beam: 37.7ft (11.5m)
Draught: 11.8ft (3.6m)
Machinery: CODAD; 4 Crossley SEMT-Pielstick 16 PA6V 280STC diesels, 28,160hp; 2 shafts, cp propellers
Speed & Range: 28kt; 4,000 miles (6,440km) at 10kt
Complement: 76
Missiles: 2 fixed quadruple launchers, Exocet MM40 medium-range SSM; 1 octuple launcher, Crotale short-range SSM
Guns: 1 OTO Melera 3in (76mm)/62 automatic gun; 2 single GAM-B01 20mm guns
ASW & USW: option for 2 triple 324mm (12.75in) torpedo tubes (not fitted at present)
Sensors: radar: Signaal MW08 air and surface search; Signaal STING and Thompson-CSF DRBV 51C fire control; Type 1007 navigation; sonar: option for ATAS active towed array (not fitted at present)
Aircraft: helicopter flightdeck

DENMARK
FFG, Niels Juel

T HE DANISH NAVY COMMISSIONED the design of these frigates via the Glasgow-based YARD bureau, although they were built in Denmark. Three ships (*Niels Juel*, *Olfert Fischer*, *Peter Tordenskiold*) were laid down in 1976, 1978 and 1979 respectively. The completion dates were 26 August 1980, 16 October 1981 and 2 April 1982.

Although there was provision for ASW torpedo tubes, these have not been fitted to date and consequently these ships have a limited ASW capability, although a hull-mounted active sonar is carried. In the surface warfare role they are much more effective, with Harpoon missiles and the OTO Melera automatic 3in (76mm) gun. The Harpoon launchers are carried just abaft the funnel, the portside set pointing aft and those on the starboard pointing forward. The 20mm guns are not always fitted. As completed, a Mk.29 octuple launcher for the Sea Sparrow SAMs was mounted on the quarter-deck aft; however all three ships have recently completed a mid-life refit in which this has been

Peter Tordenskiold *(F356)*. The Sea Sparrow VLS installation is just visible on the quarterdeck. (Maritime Photographic)

replaced by a Mk.48 modular VLS with provision for up to 12 cells, although only six are normally carried for peacetime duties. Other improvements included new communications equipment, a 3D air search radar and a new integrated combat information system.

Despite their relatively small size, these ships play a full role within NATO and at least one was deployed to the Gulf area as part of the United Nations forces involved in the 1991 war against Iraq.

Peter Tordenskiold *(F356)*, Niels Juel class frigate of the Danish Navy. (author)

SPECIFICATION

Type: FFG
Class: Niels Juel
Displacement: 1,320 tons full load
Length: 275.5ft (84m)
Beam: 33.8ft (10.3m)
Draught: 10.2ft (3.1m)
Machinery: CODOG; 1 LM2500 gas turbine, 24,600hp; 1 MTU 20V 956 TB82 diesel, 5,120hp; 2 shafts
Speed & Range: 28kt
Complement: 94
Missiles: 2 quadruple fixed launchers, Boeing Harpoon long-range SSM; 2 6-cell Mk.48 VLS launchers, Sea Sparrow short-range SAM
Guns: 1 OTO Melera 3in (76mm)/62 automatic; 4 single Oerlikon 20mm
ASW & USW: depth charges
Sensors: radar: DASA TRS-3D air search; Philips 9GR 600 surface search; Mk.95 and 9LV 200 fire control; Mil 009 navigation
Aircraft: nil

MCM, Avenger

USS Avenger (MCM 1), name ship of a class of 14 mine countermeasures vessels. (US Navy)

THE US NAVY WAS SLOW to apportion funding for modern mine warfare vessels and the 14 Avenger class ships, completed between 1987 and 1994, were a belated attempt to improve their capability in this area. The first two ships were powered by Waukesha L-1616 diesels, but problems with these led to Italian-manufactured diesels being installed in the remainder. In order to lower the ships' magnetic signature, an important attribute for a mine warfare vessel, the hull is constructed of various woods including oak, Douglas fir and Alaskan pine, although externally a thin GRP coat is applied and most of the superstructure is also GRP.

Standard Oropesa gear is carried for sweeping moored mines as well as SLQ-73 magnetic/acoustic influence sweep equipment. However, for more sophisticated work two SLQ-48 remotely operated vehicles are carried. These have a speed of up to 6kt powered by twin hydraulic motors and control is via a 4,900ft (1,500m) long cable. Each can carry cable-cutting gear or lay countermining charges. The ship's two electric motors and hydraulic bow thruster allow precise positioning and manoeuvring during minehunting operations. The last two ships (*Dextrous* and *Chief*) were completed with the British-designed NAUTIS M action information system to control minehunting operations. This equipment is now being retrofitted in the other 12 vessels.

Despite being among the largest mine warfare vessels operated by any navy, there is little room for defensive armament other than two light machine-guns. In the case of the US Navy, it can be assumed that adequate support forces will be available to cover mine clearance operations.

SPECIFICATION

Type: MCM
Class: Avenger
Displacement: 1,312 tons full load
Length: 224ft (68.3m)
Beam: 39ft (11.9m)
Draught: 12.2ft (3.7m)
Machinery: 4 Isotta Fraschini ID36 SS 6V AM diesels, 2,400hp; 2 electric motors, 400hp; 2 shafts, cp propellers; 1 hydrojet, 350hp
Speed & Range: 13.5kt
Complement: 81
Missiles: nil
Guns: 2 12.7mm (0.5in) machine-guns
ASW & USW: nil
Sensors: radar: SPS-55 surface search; SPS-66, LN66 or SPS-73 navigation; sonar: SQQ-30 or SQQ-32 high-frequency VDS active minehunting
Aircraft: nil

FS, Minerva

Danaide (F553), Minerva class corvette. (author)

THE MINERVA IS A CLASS OF EIGHT SHIPS of which the first four (*Minerva*, *Urania*, *Danaide*, *Sfinge*) were ordered in 1982 and a further four (*Driade*, *Chimera*, *Fenice*, *Sibilla*) in 1987. Plans to build more were abandoned when Italy took over the ex-Iranian Artigliere class frigates. All eight Minerva class ships were laid down between 1985 and 1989, and entered service between June 1987 and May 1991, replacing the older 800-ton Albatross class corvettes which dated from the 1950s.

Apart from purely naval roles, they are also designed to undertake offshore patrol and fishery protection tasks. In addition, the Italian Navy uses these ships to provide training for commanding officers. The normal armament is the 3in (76mm) automatic gun forward, triple ASW torpedo tubes abreast the funnel and the Aspide missile launcher aft. In addition, up to six Teseo SSM fixed launchers may be fitted in the deck space between the two superstructure blocks, although these are not fitted for normal peacetime operations.

This class is similar in concept to the Danish Niels Juel class but a reduction in size is achieved by a simpler propulsion system resulting in a slower speed. However, they are well suited to Mediterranean conditions and, as always with things Italian, they are better-looking!

SPECIFICATION

Type: FS
Class: Minerva
Displacement: 1,029 tons, 1,285 tons full load
Length: 284.1ft (86.6m)
Beam: 34.5ft (10.5m)
Draught: 10.5ft (3.2m)
Machinery: 2 Fincantieri GMT BM230.20DVM diesels, 12,600hp; 2 shafts, cp propellers
Speed & Range: 24kt; 3,500 miles (5,630km) at 18kt
Complement: 123
Missiles: 4 or 6 fixed launchers, Teseo Otomat SSM (optional); 1 Albatros octuple launcher, Aspide short-range SAM
Guns: 1 OTO Melera 3in (76mm)/62 automatic
ASW & USW: 2 triple B-515 324mm (12.75in) torpedo tubes, Mk.46 A/S torpedoes; SLQ-25 Nixie torpedo decoy
Sensors: radar: SPS-774 (RAN 10S) air and surface search; SPN-728(V)2 navigation; SPG-76 (RTN 30X) fire control; sonar: DE1167 hull-mounted active search and attack
Aircraft: nil

FSG, Eilat (Saar 5)

THE EILAT IS A JOINT US/ISRAELI DESIGN which clearly demonstrates how advances in weapons technology have allowed powerful capabilities to be built into a relatively small hull. In a complex arrangement, the ships were designed to an Israeli Navy specification by US-based John McMullen Associates Inc. and built in America by Ingalls Shipbuilding, a division of the Litton Corporation. They were then sailed to Haifa where the fitting of weapons systems and other combat equipment was carried out by Israeli Shipyards.

The final outline incorporates the latest stealth technology with flat angled surfaces covering most of the superstructure, masts and funnel. Although the main gun armament is intended to comprise a single OTO Melera 3in (76mm) automatic, the modular installation system allows it to be rapidly replaced with a Vulcan/Phalanx 20mm CIWS or a Bofors 57mm (2.2in) automatic. The 32-cell VLS silos for the indigenous Barak surface-to-air missile are positioned on the foredeck, just abaft the gun, and high up in the superstructure just abaft the funnel. The flightdeck and hangar are sized to accommodate a single Eurocopter SA 366G Dauphin or AS 565SA Sea Panther. Four of the latter have recently been delivered.

The three Eilat class ships (*Eilat*, *Lahav*, *Hanit*) are currently the largest surface combat ships in service with the Israeli Navy and were laid down in 1992 and 1993. They were subsequently completed in 1994 and 1995, although an option for a fourth ship was not exercised.

Saar 5 class corvette of the Israeli Navy.
(Mönch Archives)

Eilat *(501), lead ship of three Israeli Saar 5 class missile-armed corvettes which dramatically incorporate all the latest trends in stealth technology.*
(Maritime Photographic)

SPECIFICATION

Type: FSG
Class: Eilat (Saar 5)
Displacement: 1,075 tons standard, 1,227 tons full load
Length: 283.5ft (86.4m)
Beam: 39ft (11.9m)
Draught: 10.5ft (3.2m)
Machinery: CODOG; 1 LM2500 gas turbine, 30,000hp; 2 MTU 12V 1163 TB82 diesels, 6,600hp; 2 shafts, cp propellers
Speed & Range: 33kt; 3,500 miles (5,630km) at 17kt
Complement: 74 (inc. air detachment)
Missiles: 2 quadruple fixed launchers, Boeing Harpoon SSM; 2 32-cell VLS, Barak short-range SAM
Guns: 1 OTO Melera 3in (76mm)/62 automatic gun, or 1 Bofors 57mm (2.2in) automatic, or 1 Vulcan/Phalanx 20mm CIWS; 2 Sea Vulcan 25mm CIWS
ASW & USW: 2 triple 324mm (12.75in) torpedo tubes, Mk.46 A/S torpedoes; Rafael ATC-1 torpedo decoy
Sensors: radar: EL/M-2218S air search; SPS-55 surface search; I-band navigation; EL/M-2221 fire control; sonar: EDO Type 796 hull-mounted medium-frequency search and attack; fitted for towed array
Aircraft: 1 helicopter

MCDV, Kingston

Yellowknife (706), Kingston class marine coastal defence vessel (MCDV).
(Canadian Armed Forces)

THE KINGSTON IS A 12-SHIP CLASS BUILT by Halifax Shipyards between 1994 and 1999 following the placing of orders in 1992. The lead ship, *Kingston*, and *Glace Bay* were completed in 1996; *Nanaimo*, *Edmonton* and *Shawinigan* in 1997; *Whitehorse*, *Yellowknife*, *Goose Bay* and *Saskatoon* in 1998; *Brandon* and *Summerside* in 1999.

A feature of the design is the clear quarterdeck and well between the funnels which can accept a modularised MCM system, and one of three containerised equipment modules available can be fitted depending on the operational requirement. These comprise an SLQ-38 minesweeping module which includes single and double Oropesa sweeps for conventional moored mines, a route survey system using high-frequency sonars to map the undersea floor, and a mine inspection ROV. Apart from purely naval tasks, vessels such as these can be put to a variety of uses such as offshore patrol and fishery protection. Consequently, they are designated as maritime coast defence vessels (MCDV). The twin flat-sided funnels set well aft provide a distinctive recognition feature, and the diesel electric machinery powers the ship through two Z drives capable of 360° rotation. This allows precise control and positioning of the ship when engaged on mine warfare or survey activities.

The 12 vessels of this class are evenly distributed between Canada's Atlantic and Pacific seaboards, and are normally manned by reserve status crews.

SPECIFICATION

Type: MCDV
Class: Kingston
Displacement: 962 tons full load
Length: 181.4ft (55.3m)
Beam: 37.1ft (11.3m)
Draught: 11.2ft (3.4m)
Machinery: diesel electric; 4 Wärtsilä UD 23V12 diesels; 4 Jeumont ANR-53-50 generators; 2 Jeumont CI 560L motors, 3,000hp; 2 Z drive thrusters
Speed & Range: 15kt; 5,000 miles (8,050km) at 8kt
Complement: 31
Missiles: nil
Guns: 1 Bofors 40mm; 2 12.7mm (0.5in) machine-guns
ASW & USW: nil
Sensors: radar: Kelvin Hughes 6000 surface search; I-band navigation; sonar: high-frequency active minehunting towed side scan
Aircraft: nil

UNITED STATES
MHC, Osprey

USS Osprey (MHC-51), lead ship of a class of 12 coastal minehunters.
(Mönch Archives)

A SHORTAGE OF MINEHUNTING expertise and capability within the US Navy was highlighted during the 1991 Gulf War when the United States had to rely heavily on European navies to provide the necessary support. In the aftermath, an off-the-shelf purchase of the Italian Lerici class design, modified for US requirements, was hastily arranged. This became the Osprey class, all named after hunting birds, and in all 12 vessels were completed in US shipyards (Intermarine USA, a subsidiary of the Italian Intermarine SpA, and Avondale Industries) between 1993 and 1999.

The main change in the US version was the adoption of twin Isotta Fraschini ID36 diesels as the main propulsion machinery instead of a single Fincantieri GMT BL230 as in the Italian boats. This combination was slightly less powerful but had the advantage of standardising on the same diesel engine used in the generating sets of both vessels. The result of this was an increase in length and displacement, but otherwise the two versions were very similar in appearance.

US electronic equipment is fitted including the Raytheon/Thompson Sintra SQQ-32 minehunting sonar which is lowered from a well deck forward of the bridge. An SLQ-48 mine neutralisation system which includes an ROV is the main mine countermeasure equipment, and the twin Voith Schneider propellers with 360° thrust vectoring allow the ship to be positioned with great precision. Like the original Italian vessels, the Osprey class ships are of heavy GRP construction and the machinery is cradle-mounted and acoustically shielded to reduce noise and vibration.

SPECIFICATION

Type: MHC
Class: Osprey
Displacement: 930 tons full load
Length: 188ft (57.3m)
Beam: 35.9ft (11m)
Draught: 9.5ft (2.9m)
Machinery: 2 Isotta Fraschini ID36 SS 8V AM diesels, 1,600hp; 2 Voith Schneider propellers; 3 Isotta Fraschini ID36 diesel generators, 984kW
Speed & Range: 10kt; 1,500 miles (2,410km) at 10kt
Complement: 51
Missiles: nil
Guns: 2 12.7mm (0.5in) machine-guns
ASW & USW: nil
Sensors: radar: SPS 64(V)9 surface search; R41XX navigation; sonar: SQQ-32 VDS high-frequency minehunting
Aircraft: nil

MCMV, Hunt

HMS Berkeley *(M40), Hunt class MCMV.*
(author)

THE 13 HUNT CLASS MCMVs form the backbone of the Royal Navy's mine warfare flotillas and have seen considerable service in many operational theatres since the lead ship, HMS *Brecon*, commissioned in March 1980. At that time she was the largest GRP vessel afloat, the technique having been pioneered by Vosper Thornycroft with the Ton class coastal minesweeper HMS *Wilton*, which was launched in January 1972. The remaining 12 Hunt class ships commissioned between 1981 and 1989, and all were built by Vosper Thornycroft at its Woolston yard.

As originally completed they were armed with a single 40mm Bofors gun but this was later replaced by the faster-firing DS 30B 30mm. The additional 20mm guns are normally only fitted when the ships deploy to operational tasks. Eight of these ships deployed to the Persian Gulf in 1990/91 in support of the Desert Shield/Desert Storm operations and between them provided a major component of the allied mine countermeasures, and destroyed over 200 mines. These ships carry Oropesa wire sweep gear for conventional mines, a towed acoustic generator and an MS14 magnetic loop, as well as two French-designed PAP 104 ROVs. With this sophisticated array of equipment, backed up by high-definition minehunting sonars, they are able to detect and deal with virtually every type of mine in existence today.

However, such capabilities do not come cheaply, and subsequently the Royal Navy moved on to the Sandown class of single role minehunters, intended for a much more limited range of tasks. In the meantime, some of the Hunts have undergone a limited mid-life update which includes the provision of PAP 104 able to operate down to depths of 1,000ft (305m). Three ships, *Cottesmore*, *Dulverton* and *Brecon*, are serving as patrol ships off Northern Ireland and carry two RIBs instead of the conventional sweep gear, which has been temporarily removed.

SPECIFICATION

Type: MCMV
Class: Hunt
Displacement: 750 tons full load
Length: 197ft (57.6m)
Beam: 32.8ft (10m)
Draught: 11.2ft (3.4m) maximum
Machinery: 2 Ruston-Paxman 9-59K Deltic diesels, 1,900 hp; 1 9-55B Deltic diesel generator and auxiliary drive, 780 hp; 2 shafts; bow thruster
Speed & Range: 15kt; 1,730 miles (2,780km) at 12kt
Complement: 45
Missiles: nil
Guns: 1 DS 30B 30mm; 2 single GAM-CO1 20mm; 2 7.62mm (0.303in) machine-guns
Sensors: radar: Type 10-06 or 1007 navigation; sonar: Plessey 193M hull-mounted minehunting; Mil Cross hull-mounted active mine avoidance; Type 2059 tracking
Aircraft: nil

FSG, Laksamana

Above and right: Laksamana Hang Nadim (F134), one of a class of four modern fast corvettes built in Italy for the Malaysian Navy. (Guy Toremans)

THIS CLASS OF SIX VERY POWERFUL fast attack craft was originally completed in Italy for Iraq in 1988. However, by that date the UN had imposed an embargo on arms sales to Iraq and they were laid up, awaiting a resolution of their fate. Eventually they were sold to Malaysia, and, following refits, the first pair (*Laksamana Hang Nadim, Laksamana Tun Abdul Gamil*) were commissioned in 1997 and the other two (*Laksamana Muhammad Amin, Laksamana Tun Pusman*) in 1999. Two further units, for which Iraq has paid in full, remain laid up in Italy, and these differ from the Malaysian vessels in that they have a hangar and flightdeck fitted aft instead of the missile launchers and the twin 40mm mounting. They are unlikely ever to be delivered.

The four Malaysian vessels carry an armament which would not be out of place on a frigate of three or four times the displacement. Packed into the 700 tons is potent anti-ship armament in the shape of Teseo SSMs and the 3in (76mm) automatic gun, an excellent defence capability against air and missile attack, and a respectable ASW outfit. These are backed up by an integrated combat information and weapons control suite, almost all produced by the Italian electronics company Selenia.

Although these boats were probably obtained at less than the cost of new construction, they nevertheless placed a strain on the navy's budget and the running costs will be greater than normal due to the fact that most of the weapons systems and electronics are not fitted to other Malaysian ships, resulting in the need to maintain additional stockpiles of spares and ammunition.

SPECIFICATION

Type: FSG
Class: Laksamana
Displacement: 705 tons full load
Length: 204.4ft (62.3m)
Beam: 30.5ft (9.3m)
Draught: 8ft (2.5m)
Machinery: 4 MTU 20V 956 TB92 diesels, 20,120hp; 4 shafts
Speed & Range: 36kt; 2,300 miles (3,700km) at 18kt
Complement: 47
Missiles: 6 fixed single launchers, OTO Melera Teseo Mk.2 long-range SSM; 1 4-cell Albatros launcher, Aspide short-range SAM
Guns: 1 OTO Melera 3in (76mm)/62 automatic; 1 twin Breda 40mm CIWS
ASW & USW: 2 ILAS3 triple 324mm (12.75in) torpedo tubes, A244S A/S torpedoes
Sensors: radar: RAN 12L/X air and surface search; Type 1007 navigation; RTN 10X and RTN 20X fire control
Aircraft: nil

MHC/MSC, Lerici/Gaeta

A flotilla of Lerici class minehunters of the Italian Navy.
(Marina Militare, Italy)

THE ORIGINAL FOUR LERICI CLASS minehunters (*Lerici*, *Sapri*, *Milazzo*, *Vieste*) were ordered in 1978 and all were subsequently commissioned in 1985. These all featured GRP construction with the main machinery on anti-vibration mountings, while the engines themselves used non-magnetic materials as much as possible. These measures combined to reduce the ships' acoustic and magnetic signatures. The ships were fitted for both conventional minesweeping with Oropesa gear and for more sophisticated minehunting using a remotely operated vehicle (ROV). In addition, there were facilities for divers including equipment stowage and a decompression chamber (significantly, the complement of 47 officers and men includes no fewer than seven divers).

The follow-on Gaeta class ships (*Gaeta*, *Termoli*, *Alghero*, *Numana*, *Crotone*, *Viareggio*, *Chioggia*, *Rimini*) were ordered in two batches in 1988 and 1991 and were subsequently completed between 1992 and 1996. These differed from the earlier Lerici class ships in that the hull was lengthened by approximately 20ft (6m) with a consequent rise in displacement. This was mainly the result of fitting a third hydraulic thruster, but other improvements included an improved sonar system for minehunting, more electrical generating capacity, an upgraded ROV and several other improvements in equipment and systems. Many of these were subsequently applied to the Lerici class as they were refitted.

This design has done well on the export market with sales of four ships to Malaysia and two to Nigeria. In addition, modified versions have been produced in the United States (12), Australia (6) and Thailand (2, plus options on 6 more).

SPECIFICATION

Type: MHC/MSC
Class: Lerici/Gaeta
Displacement: 697 tons full load
Length: 172.1ft (52.5m)
Beam: 32.5ft (9.9m)
Draught: 8.6ft (2.6m)
Machinery: 1 Fincantieri GMT BL230.8M diesel, 1,985hp; 1 shaft, cp propeller; 3 Isotta Fraschini ID36 SS6V diesels, 1,481hp; 3 hydraulic 360° rotating propellers
Speed & Range: 14kt; 1,500 miles (2,415km) at 14kt
Complement: 47
Missiles: nil
Guns: 2 Oerlikon 20mm
ASW & USW: Pluto RPV mine destruction system
Sensors: radar: SPN-728(V)3 navigation; sonar: FIAR SQQ-14(T) VDS classification and survey
Aircraft: nil
(Note: data applies to the Gaeta class)

SWEDEN
FSG, Visby

U NDER RECENTLY ANNOUNCED PLANS, the surface combat element of the Swedish Navy will comprise two Stockholm class and four Göteborg class corvettes built between 1982 and 1993, as well as six of the revolutionary Visby class corvettes which will incorporate all the latest elements of stealth technology. The design is based on experience gained with the catamaran-hulled trials vessel *Smyge* launched in 1991 and now decommissioned. An order for the first two Visby class corvettes was placed in 1995, and a second pair was ordered in December 1996. The lead ship was launched in mid-2000 and all four will be in service by March 2006.

The design of the ship uses the now familiar flat angled surface for the hull and superstructure, with the former being of GRP construction while all surfaces are coated with radar-absorbent material (RAM). All deck-mounted equipment such as the gun and masts will be designed to reduce emissions or reflections while as much equipment as possible will be in concealed positions so that, overall, the ship will have exceptionally clean lines. A single Agusta Bell AB 206 Jet Ranger will be carried initially, but the Swedish Navy is actively seeking a more capable replacement helicopter. Some of the equipment developed for the Visby class will also be fitted to the two Stockholm class ships when they undergo a modernisation refit, to be completed by 2002. This will include new Allied Signal TF50A gas turbines, a Celsius CETRIS combat management system, ESM equipment and an automated bridge control system.

The Visby class is attracting much attention from the world's navies and Singapore has already expressed an interest in purchasing vessels of a similar design.

Above and below: Artist impressions of the Visby class stealth corvettes now under construction for the Swedish Navy. (CelsiusTech)

The Stockholm class corvettes will remain in service alongside the new Visby class. (CelsiusTech)

SPECIFICATION

Type: FSG
Class: Visby
Displacement: 620 tons full load
Length: 236.2m (72m)
Beam: 34.1ft (10.4m)
Draught: 8.2ft (2.5m)
Machinery: CODOG; 4 Allied Signal TF50A gas turbines, 21,760hp; 2 MTU 16VN90 diesels, 3,536hp; 2 Kamewa water jets; bow thruster
Speed & Range: 35kt
Complement: 43
Missiles: 8 RBS-15 Mk.II SSM
Guns: 1 Bofors 57mm (2.2in)/70 SAK Mk.3
ASW & USW: 4 fixed 400mm (15.75in) torpedo tubes
Sensors: radar: Sea Giraffe 3D air and surface search; I-band surface search; J-band fire control; sonar: CDC Hydra bow-mounted high-frequency active search and attack; active VDS; passive towed array
Aircraft: 1 helicopter

FRANCE, GERMANY, BELGIUM, THE NETHERLANDS
MHC, Éridan (Tripartite)

A VERY SUCCESSFUL international collaborative programme which resulted in a total of 39 ships being completed for no fewer than five navies. The original partners were Belgium, France and The Netherlands, each of whom intended to build 15 ships, although the Belgian and French orders were subsequently reduced to 10 each. Pakistan ordered three ships, of which the first was actually the last of the French order, and two additional ships were built at Lorient and Karachi. Another French vessel was ordered to replace the one sold to Pakistan in 1992, and subsequently the French Navy acquired a further three from Belgium in 1997, bringing the total in service to 13. The Netherlands Navy took delivery of 15 Tripartite minehunters and built two more to a slightly modified design for Indonesia.

In the original construction programme each country built and fitted out its own ships with Belgium providing all electrical systems, France the minehunting equipment and some electronics and The Netherlands the machinery. In addition to mechanical and acoustic minesweeping gear, these minehunters carried two PAP 104 remotely operated underwater vehicles which destroyed mines by laying charges alongside them. The Netherlands Navy is now actively working on an upgrade of its minehunters which will involve the fitting of new minehunting sonars and command/control systems, as well as a new mine disposal system to replace the PAP 104s which lack the sophistication to deal with the latest mines. In addition, they will be converted to act as mother ships for remotely controlled Troika drones carrying acoustic and magnetic sweeping gear. A similar concept is already operational with the German and Danish navies.

Orion (M645), a French Navy Éridan class Tripartite minehunter.
(Marine Nationale, France)

Mine clearance operations in progress by the French minehunter Lyre (M648).
(Marine Nationale, France)

SPECIFICATION

Type: MHC
Class: Éridan (Tripartite)
Displacement: 562 tons standard, 605 tons full load
Length: 168.9ft (51.5m)
Beam: 29.2ft (8.9m)
Draught: 8.2ft (2.5m)
Machinery: 1 Stork Wärtsilä A-RUB 215X-12 diesel, 1,860hp; 1 shaft, cp propeller; 2 auxiliary motors, 240hp; active rudders; bow thruster
Speed & Range: 15kt; 3,000 miles (4,830km) at 12kt
Complement: 46
Missiles: nil
Guns: 1 Giat 20F2 20mm and 1 12.7mm (0.5in) machine-gun
ASW & USW: nil
Sensors: radar: Racal Decca 1229 navigation; sonar: DUBM 21B or 21D hull-mounted high-frequency active
Aircraft: nil

FSG, Victory

Valour *(P89)*, first of a class of six fast corvettes whose imposing appearance belies their relatively small size. (Maritime Photographic)

THESE WELL-ARMED CRAFT are based on the Lürssen MGB62 design, and the lead ship, *Victory*, was built in Germany for delivery to Singapore in 1990. Another five (*Valour*, *Vigilance*, *Valiant*, *Vigour*, *Vengeance*) were completed by Singapore SB and Marine between 1990 and 1991.

The most distinctive feature of these ships is the tall square-sectioned mast amidships which carries the antenna for most of the EW and ESM equipment installed, as well as the rotating scanner for the Ericsson Sea Giraffe search radar. Immediately fore and aft of the mast are the two parabolic aerials forming part of the Elta fire control radar systems which provide control channels for the 3in (76mm) automatic gun and the Barak surface-to-air missiles. The latter are fired from twin 8-cell VLS silos set into the stern and flanking the VDS installation and were fitted as part of a modernisation programme started in 1996/97.

Further vessels based on the Lürssen design have been sold to Bahrain and the United Arab Emirates, but in both cases a substantial deckhouse topped by a helicopter flightdeck has been erected on the afterdeck and the anti-submarine capability deleted. The Bahrain vessels, *Al Manama* and *Al Muharraq*, were delivered in 1997 and 1998, and are armed with a 3in (76mm) automatic gun, a twin 40mm right aft and two single 20mm in the bridge wings, as well as four fixed Exocet launchers amidships. A single Bölkow 105 helicopter is embarked, although it carries no armament. The two UAE vessels form the Muray Jib class, and were completed in 1990 and 1991 with a more sophisticated armament including a Crotale missile launcher on the stern and a Goalkeeper CIWS

high up abaft the mast, as well as the standard 3in (76mm) gun and Exocet missiles. The helicopter in this case is an Aérospatiale Alouette, used for reconnaissance only.

SPECIFICATION

Type: FSG
Class: Victory
Displacement: 595 tons full load
Length: 204.7ft (62.4m)
Beam: 27.9ft (8.5m)
Draught: 10.2ft (3.1m)
Machinery: 4 MTU 16V 538 TB93 diesels, 15,020hp; 4 shafts
Speed & Range: 35kt; 4,000 miles (6,440km) at 18kt
Complement: 49
Missiles: 2 fixed quadruple launchers, Boeing Harpoon long-range SSM; 2 8-cell VLS, Rafale/Barak short-range SAM
Guns: 1 OTO Melera 3in (76mm)/62 automatic; 4 12.7mm (0.5in) machine-guns
ASW & USW: 2 B515 triple 324mm (12.75in) torpedo tubes, A244S A/S torpedoes
Sensors: radar: Sea Giraffe surface search; Type 1007 navigation; EL/M-2221 fire control; sonar: TSM 2064 VDS active search and attack
Aircraft: nil

DENMARK
PG/MHC, Flyvefisken

THE STANDARDFLEX 300 is a very interesting concept in which a small high-powered hull can be adapted for a wide variety of roles by fitting modular weapons systems and equipment. The modules are all built to a standard size and are completely interchangeable in a matter of hours, imparting a degree of flexibility which offers increased combat effectiveness while significantly reducing costs – an important consideration for relatively small navies.

These modules can be installed in four separate wells, one on the foredeck and the other on the long and unobstructed quarterdeck aft of the super-structure and funnel. In most variants the forward well is occupied by a single OTO Melera 3in (76mm) automatic gun, but other modules include a sextuple Sea Sparrow SAM launcher, twin torpedo tubes for FFV Type 613 21in (533mm) wire-guided homing torpedoes, mine countermeasures equipment, a variable depth sonar, a rigid inflatable boat and associated equipment, a crane and pollution control equipment. Each module has a standard-sized base with common connectors for the ship's services such as power supplies, water, electronic and data transfer links. Within the ship itself, considerable automation of systems and machinery is utilised to allow operation by a small complement, the size of which varies according to the role.

The Standardflex can be adapted to perform several roles including air and surface combat, mine countermeasures, minelaying, patrol and surveillance, anti-pollution, disaster relief and oceanographic survey. In carrying out these tasks, the 14 Flyvefisken class ships completed between 1989 and 1993 have replaced no fewer than 22 vessels of three distinct types in Danish naval service.

When employed in the MHC role, the Standardflex 300 can act as mother ship for two unmanned surface auxiliary vessels (SAV). The original versions displaced 32 tons and basically acted as platforms to deploy a minehunting sonar into unsanitised areas. Six of these were built, but these will be supplemented by up to 16 modified SAVs which are much larger (125 tons) and can be utilised, with crews, for other tasks. The first of these was delivered in 1999 and the building programme will continue to 2006.

Flyvefisken (P550), first of the innovative Danish Standardflex 300 multi-role warships. (CelsiusTech)

Flyvefisken class /SF300
Number of ships: 14
Length: 54 m
Displacement: 300 tonnes

Drawing, Standardflex 300. (CelsiusTech)

SPECIFICATION

Type: PG/MHC
Class: Flyvefisken
Displacement: 480 tons, full load
Length: 177.2ft (29.5m)
Beam: 29.5ft (9m)
Draught: 8.2ft (2.5m)
Machinery: CODAG; 1 LM2500 gas turbine 5,450hp, centre shaft; 2 MTU 16V 396TB94 diesels, 5,800 hp, outer shafts; hydraulic auxiliary propulsion
Speed & Range: 30kt; 2,400 miles (3,860km) at 18kt
Complement: 29 (max.)
Missiles: 2 quadruple fixed launchers, Boeing Harpoon SSM; Up to 3 Mk.48 twin launchers, Sea Sparrow SAM
Guns: 1 OTO Melera 3in (76mm)/62 automatic; 2 12.7mm (0.5in) machine-guns
ASW & USW: 1 twin 21in (533mm) torpedo tubes, FFV Type 613 wire-guided torpedoes; 60 mines
Sensors: radar: AWS 6 or TRS-3D air and surface search; Terma Scanta Mil surface search; Furuno navigation; Celsius Tech 9LV200 fire control; sonar: Celsius Tech CTS-36/39 hull-mounted active search; TSM 2640 Salmon VDS
Aircraft: nil

A Modified SAV Class which can act as a remotely controlled unmanned drone under the direction of a parent Standardflex 300. (Danyard Aalborg)

MHC, Sandown

THE SANDOWN CLASS SHIPS ARE DESIGNATED as single role minehunters (SRMH) to indicate that they are not equipped with traditional minesweeping gear but rely on sophisticated sonar systems to locate various types of mines whose destruction is effected by a remote-control mine disposal system (RCMDS) based on two PAP 104 Mk.5 ROVs.

The first ship, HMS *Sandown*, was ordered in 1985 and completed in 1989. She was followed by a further batch of four vessels (*Inverness*, *Cromer*, *Walney*, *Bridport*) which commissioned between January 1991 and November 1993. However, orders for further examples were continually deferred for political and financial reasons and were not placed until 1994, resulting in five ships, *Penzance* and *Pembroke* in 1998, *Grimsby* in 1999 and *Bangor* and *Ramsey* in 2000. The final two units, *Blythe* and *Shoreham*, are due to commission in 2001.

These later ships feature a number of improvements including larger vectored thrust propellers, improved diver facilities and a new crane for handling the ROVs. In common with most modern minehunters, the Sandown class ships are of GRP construction and feature vectored thrust propellers and a bow thruster in order to allow precise positioning over the seabed. All 12 ships were built by Vosper Thornycroft at its Woolston yard, and in service they are all allocated to the 3rd MCM squadron. A further three ships were built by Vosper Thornycroft for Saudi Arabia, and these were delivered in 1991, 1993 and 1997. These are essentially similar to the Royal Navy vessels, but carry twin 30mm gun mountings on the forecastle.

A class of four similar vessels was completed by Bazán for the Spanish Navy in 1999/2000. At 530 tons full load, they are slightly larger than the RN vessels, and a further batch of four ships is expected to be ordered.

Above and below left: HMS Sandown *(M101), single role minehunter. (Royal Navy)*

SPECIFICATION

Type: MHC
Class: Sandown
Displacement: 450 tons standard, 484 tons full load
Length: 172.2ft (52.5m)
Beam: 34.4ft (10.5m)
Draught: 7.5ft (2.3m)
Machinery: 2 Paxman Valenta 6RP200E diesels, 1,523hp; Voith Schneider propulsion; bow thrusters
Speed & Range: 13 kt; 3,000 miles (4,830km) at 12kt
Complement: 34
Missiles: nil
Guns: 1 DS30B 30mm gun
ASW & USW: nil
Sensors: radar: Type 1007 navigation; sonar: Marconi Type 2093 multi-function VDS minehunting
Aircraft: nil

PCFG, Barzan (Vita)

THESE ARE FAST AND POWERFUL BOATS based on Vosper Thornycroft's 184ft (56m) Vita design. Although displacing only around 350 tons (standard), their gun and missile armament compares favourably with many much larger ships. A sophisticated EW suite is installed which includes Thompson CSF DR3000S ESM equipment, chaff and IR decoy flares, and Dassault Salamandre ARBB 33 ECM jamming transmitters. Despite Vosper's expertise with GRP construction, these craft have steel hulls and aluminium superstructure. The four-shaft layout is unusual in modern warships, but in a small craft it does away with the requirement for heavy and complex gearboxes and also ensures considerable redundancy in a combat damage situation. There are two separate machinery spaces which can operate independently of each other and the whole installation, including electrical generation and auxiliary systems, can be controlled by one person on the bridge using a colour VDU console.

The four Qatari vessels (*Barzan, Huwar, Al Udeid, Al Debeel*) were ordered in 1993 and they were subsequently laid down at six-month intervals from February 1994. The first three were then commissioned in 1996 and the last vessel in July 1997.

The Vita design is based on fast patrol vessels built for Kenya (two craft delivered 1987) and Oman (four Dhofar class ships were delivered 1982–89). These had a similar armament but were powered by four Paxman Valenta diesels and were capable of 38–40kt. In the Vita class vessels, the hull is modified by increasing the freeboard amidships and this, together with a slight increase in beam, allows an additional accommodation deck.

*Al Udeid **and** Al Debeel**, two Barzan class fast attack craft of the Qatar Emeri Navy. (Vosper Thornycroft)***

SPECIFICATION

Type: PCFG
Class: Barzan (Vita)
Displacement: 450 tons full load
Length: 185ft (56m)
Beam: 29.5ft (9m)
Draught: 8.2ft (2.5m)
Machinery: 4 MTU 20V 538 TB93 diesels, 18,740hp; 4 shafts
Speed & Range: 35kt; in excess of 1,800 miles (2,900km) at 12kt
Complement: 35
Missiles: 2 quadruple fixed launchers, Exocet MM40 SSM; 1 sextuple launcher, Mistral short-range SAM
Guns: 1 OTO Melera 3in (76mm)/62 automatic gun; 1 Goalkeeper 7-barrelled 30mm CIWS; 2 12.7mm (0.5in) machine-guns
ASW & USW: nil
Sensors: radar: Thompson-CSF MRR air and surface search; Signaal STING fire control; Type 1007 navigation
Aircraft: nil

FINLAND
PCFG, Rauma

THIS CLASS OF FOUR FAST ATTACK craft was completed by Finnish shipyards between 1990 and 1992 and is a development of the Helsinki class built during the 1980s. They are primarily intended for the anti-ship role and a combination of high speed and relatively shallow draught make them ideal for Baltic operations.

The propulsion system incorporates Italian-designed water jets instead of propellers, again assisting operation in shallow waters. A hull-mounted sonar and lightweight towed array, backed up by A/S mortars and depth charges, gives a limited anti-submarine capability and serves at least to discourage hostile submarine activity. The aft-mounted Mistral SAMs can be replaced by a twin 23mm gun mounting at short notice. Saab RBS 15SF missiles provide the main anti-ship capability and up to six are normally carried on fixed launcher containers, although there is provision for a maximum of eight.

Further development of the Rauma class has resulted in the Hamina fast attack craft, which is slightly larger and similar in outline and armament but the superstructure and gun mounting follows the latest stealth technology style, being made up of multi-faceted flat surfaces constructed from composite materials. The first of these was ordered in 1996 and completed in 1998, although plans for further vessels of this type do not appear to be proceeding.

Rauma (70), one of a class of four fast attack craft built in Finland.
(Maritime Photographic)

SPECIFICATION

Type: PCFG
Class: Rauma
Displacement: 215 tons standard, 248 tons full load
Length: 157.5ft (48m)
Beam: 26.2ft (8m)
Draught: 4.5ft (1.5m)
Machinery: 2 MTU 16V 538 TB93 diesels, 7,500hp; 2 water jets
Speed & Range: 30kt
Complement: 19
Missiles: 6 single fixed launchers, Saab RBS 15SF long-range SSM; 1 sextuple launcher, Matra Mistral short range SAM
Guns: 1 Bofors 40mm/70; 2 12.7mm (0.5in) machine-guns
ASW & USW: 4 9-barrelled LLS-920 A/S mortars; depth charges
Sensors: radar: 9GA 208 surface search; Bofors 9LV 225 fire control; ARPA navigation; sonar: Toadfish high-frequency active search and attack; low-frequency passive towed array
Aircraft: nil

AMPHIBIOUS WARFARE VESSELS

ONE OF THE GREAT advantages of seapower is the ability to transport and land military forces on any suitable stretch of coastline. Amphibious operations matured during World War II when huge fleets of specialist vessels and craft were built to facilitate the island-hopping campaign in the Pacific and the great set-piece invasions of North Africa, Sicily, Italy and Normandy in Europe. The tradition continued in Korea during the 1950s, and recent events have only served to emphasise the importance of this type of operation.

All major navies aspire to an amphibious capability and today this is achieved by a variety of purpose-built ships. The helicopter has transformed the nature of amphibious operations, being first tried out by the British and French during the Suez operation of 1956. Although this was a political disaster, the military operation was impressive and

gave birth to the concept of a dedicated commando carrier or landing platform helicopter (LPH). These look very similar to aircraft carriers and have a full-length flightdeck. Indeed, some are able to operate fixed-wing aircraft if required. The other major amphibious warfare vessel is the LSD (landing ship dock), a major vessel equipped to carry troops and equipment as well as the landing craft to carry them ashore. These normally have a large flightdeck aft to allow the operation of helicopters, and some of the latest designs incorporate a full-length flightdeck, although they do not normally have the hangar facilities of a dedicated LPH.

Examples of both types of major amphibious warfare vessels are included in this section, although space does not permit the inclusion of the numerous specialised landing craft which are an integral part of any amphibious operation.

UNITED STATES
LHD, Wasp

USS Essex (LHD-2), Wasp class amphibious assault ship.
(US Navy)

THE US MARINE CORPS HAS A LONG and proud history, but its reputation was forged in the great amphibious operations across the Pacific during World War II. Since that time it has continually developed tactics, weapons and equipment in order to maintain the capability to put US troops ashore, under opposition, in any part of the world.

The most important component in such actions are the large helicopter-carrying landing ships of which the Wasp class is the latest and most powerful. A development of the earlier Tarawa class, there are currently six of these large and very capable amphibious assault ships in service, with a seventh (*Iwo Jima*) due for completion in February 2001, and an eighth was authorised in 2000. The first of class, USS *Wasp*, was laid down in 1985 and completed in 1989, and the remainder were commissioned as follows: *Essex* 1992, *Kearsage* 1993, *Boxer* 1995, *Bataan* 1997 and *Bonhomme Richard* 1998.

Each can carry around 1,800 troops, equivalent to three battalions, together with their stores and vehicles, including main battle tanks. These can be ferried ashore in three LCACs (large hovercraft) or 12 conventional LCMs, all of which can be accommodated within an internal well dock measuring 267ft by 50ft (81m by 15m). This is accessed through the stern. There is also provision for no fewer than 42 CH-46E Sea Knight helicopters, although any helicopter in the US Navy or Marine inventory can be operated, including the massive CH-53D Sea Stallion. A detachment of six or eight AV-8B Harriers is usually embarked to provide close air support, but the Wasp class ships can also act as conventional support carriers, in which case the air group would comprise 20 Harriers and four to six SH-60B Seahawk helicopters. Unusually for large modern warships, the propulsion machinery is conventional oil-fired boilers and steam turbines. A sophisticated combat data system is fitted including the integrated tactical amphibious warfare data system (ITAWDS) and the marine tactical amphibious C² system (MTACCS), as well as various tactical and SATCOM links, enabling these ships to act as command platforms for amphibious operations.

SPECIFICATION

Type: LHD
Class: Wasp
Displacement: 28,233 tons standard, 40,532 tons full load
Length: 844ft (257.3m)
Beam: oa 140.1ft (42.7m), wl 106ft (32.3m)
Draught: 26.6ft (8.1m)
Machinery: steam turbine; 2 Westinghouse turbines, 70,000hp; 2 shafts
Speed & Range: 22kt; 9,500 miles (15,290km) at 18kt
Complement: 1,077 + troops
Missiles: 2 Mk.29 octuple launchers, Sea Sparrow SAM; 2 Mk.49 multiple launchers, RAM short-range SAM
Guns: 2 or 3 Vulcan/Phalanx 6-barrelled 20mm CIWS
ASW & USW: SLQ-25 Nixie torpedo decoy
Sensors: radar: SPS-48E long-range 3D air search; SPS-49 air search; Mk.23 target acquisition; SPS-67 surface search; SPS-64(V)9 navigation; SPN-35A and SPN-43B aircraft control; Mk.95 fire control
Aircraft: 6–8 (max. 20) fixed-wing, 42 helicopters

UNITED STATES
LHA, Tarawa

THE DEVELOPMENT OF VIABLE troop-carrying helicopters in the decade following World War II led to the concept of a new type of amphibious assault ship in which helicopters supplemented or replaced traditional landing craft. Although early examples were converted conventional aircraft carriers, the US Navy laid down the first purpose-designed ships in 1958. This was the Iwo Jima class, displacing some 18,000 tons at full load and carrying a marine battalion together with up to 20 helicopters. Seven ships were completed between 1961 and 1970, but all have now been retired. Their successors were the five Tarawa class ships, of which the name ship entered service in 1976, followed by *Saipan* (1977), *Belleau Wood* (1978), *Nassau* (1979) and *Peleliu* (1980).

These are much more capable ships than their predecessors and were intended to replace both the helicopter assault carrier and the landing ship dock (LSD). As well as embarking 26 CH-46 Sea Knight or 19 CH-53D Sea Stallion helicopters, these ships also accommodate four LCU 1610 landing craft (or greater numbers of smaller craft) in a 268ft by 78ft (81m by 24m) docking well accessed via a stern gate when flooded. Approximately 1,700 troops can be embarked together with all their vehicles, stores and equipment. For close air support, up to six AV-8B Harriers can be embarked instead of some of the helicopters.

Although now over 20 years old, these ships have been constantly updated and are fitted with ACDS (advanced combat direction system) and ITAWDS, as found in the later Wasp class, while other improvements include new radars and communications equipment as well as RAM missiles and Vulcan/

USS **Belleau Wood** *(LHA-3), Tarawa class LHA.* *(Maritime Photographic)*

Phalanx CIWS for close-range self-defence. The three 5in (127mm) guns fitted as part of the original armament were removed in 1997/98.

SPECIFICATION

Type: LHA
Class: Tarawa
Displacement: 40,000 tons full load
Length: 834ft (254.2m)
Beam: 131.9ft (40.2m)
Draught: 25.9ft (7.9m)
Machinery: steam turbine; 2 Westinghouse turbines, 70,000hp; 2 shafts; bow thruster
Speed & Range: 24kt; 10,000 miles (16,100km) at 20kt
Complement: 930 + troops
Missiles: 2 Mk.49 multiple launchers, RAM short-range SAM
Guns: 2 Vulcan/Phalanx 6-barrelled 20mm CIWS; 6 single 25mm guns; 8 12.7mm (0.5in) machine-guns
ASW & USW: SLQ-25 Nixie torpedo decoy
Sensors: radar: SPS-48E and SPS-40E air search; Mk.23 target acquisition; SPS-67(v)3 surface search; SPS-64 navigation; SPN-35A and SPN-43B aircraft control; SPG-60 and SPQ-9A fire control
Aircraft: 6 fixed-wing, 26 helicopters (max.)

LPD, San Antonio

THE SAN ANTONIO (LPD-17) CLASS represents an important step forward in the consolidation and modernisation of the US Navy's amphibious forces for the 21st century. Two ships (*San Antonio* and *New Orleans*) are currently under construction for completion in 2002 and 2004, but it is anticipated that a total of 12 will be in service by 2009. The initial contract was awarded in December 1996 to an industrial alliance led by Avondale with Bath Iron Works and Raytheon Company to design and construct the first of an anticipated 12 ships under the navy's LPD-17 programme. Avondale will build the first of class ship and the second, and Bath would construct the third. When all are in service they will have replaced no fewer than four different classes of existing ships including the three Anchorage class LSD, two Newport class LST and the Austin class LPDs.

The mission of the LPD-17 ships is to transport marines, with helicopters and air-cushioned landing craft, to troublespots around the world. The ship is of all-steel construction with diesel propulsion. The design provides three vehicle decks of 25,402 sq. ft (2,340 sq. m) and two cargo holds with 25,548 cu. ft (723 cu. m) for bulk cargo and ammunition magazines, in addition to 43,600 cu. ft (1,234 cu. m) for cargo fuel. Accommodation is provided for two LCAC (landing craft air-cushioned) in the aft well deck, while 720 troops and 15 vehicles can be embarked. At the stern of the ship the landing deck is able to accommodate two Sikorsky CH-53E Sea Stallion helicopters, four Bell AH/UH-1 Iroquois twin Huey helicopters, four Boeing CH-46 Sea Knight helicopters or two Bell V-22 Osprey tilt-rotor aircraft. The hangar deck provides aviation maintenance facilities and is sufficiently large to accommodate one Sea Stallion, two Sea Knights, three Iroquois helicopters or one Osprey tilt-rotor aircraft. The hangar doors are constructed by Indal Technologies. Each blast-resistant door weighs 39,700lb (18,000kg) and has three horizontal folding panels. The combination of LCACs and helicopters, to the exclusion of conventional landing craft, will allow the rapid deployment ashore of the embarked marines.

Computer images of the San Antonio class (LPD-17) now under construction.
(Litton Industries)

SPECIFICATION

Type: LPD
Class: San Antonio (LPD-17)
Displacement: 25,300 tons full load
Length: 683.7ft (208.4m)
Beam: 104.7ft (31.9m)
Draught: 23ft (7m)
Machinery: 4 Colt-Pielstick PC2.5 diesels, 40,000hp; 2 shafts, cp propellers
Speed & Range: 22kt
Complement: 362 + troops
Missiles: 2 8-cell Mk.41 VLS, Evolved Sea Sparrow SAM; 2 Mk.31 launchers, RAM short-range SAM
Guns: 3 single 25mm or 30mm; 4 12.7mm (0.5in) machine-guns
ASW & USW: SLQ-25A Nixie towed decoy
Sensors: radar: SPS-48E air search; SPS-73 surface search; SPQ-9B fire control
Aircraft: up to 6 helicopters

LPH, Ocean

ALTHOUGH TENDERS FOR THIS VESSEL were invited in 1987 by the UK Ministry of Defence, it was not until May 1993 that an order was placed with Vickers Shipbuilding and Engineering Ltd (now BAE Systems) in Barrow in Furness, Cumbria. HMS *Ocean* eventually commissioned in September 1998 when it provided a significant boost to the Royal Navy's amphibious capabilities, its role being to achieve the rapid landing of an assault force by helicopter and landing craft.

The hull design is based on that of the Invincible class aircraft carriers (also built by Vickers) with a modified superstructure. The building schedule included hull construction by Kvaerner Govan on the River Clyde and sailing under its own power to the BAE Systems shipyards at Barrow in Furness for the fitting of military equipment. As completed, the ship carries a crew of 255, an aircrew of 206 and 480 marines. An additional 320 marines could be accommodated in a short-term emergency. HMS *Ocean* is capable of transporting and sustaining an embarked military force of up to 800 men equipped with artillery, vehicles and stores. The ship has the capacity for 40 vehicles but is not designed to land heavy tanks. There are four LCVP Mk.5 landing craft on davits. There are also full facilities for 12 EH101 Merlin and six Lynx helicopters, and landing and refuelling facilities for Chinook helicopters. Twenty Sea Harriers could be carried, but not supported. The flightdeck is served by two aircraft lifts. HMS *Ocean* is equipped with the BAE Systems ADAWS 2000 combat data system, Link 11, 14 and 16 communications, a Matra Marconi SATCOM 1D satellite communications system and a Merlin computer link. The ADAWS 2000 combat data system, installed on both HMS *Ocean* and on the Royal Navy's landing platform dock assault ship, is compatible with other ships of the Royal Navy's front-line fleet.

Almost from the moment she entered service in 1998, HMS *Ocean* has proved her worth. On an early trials cruise to the West Indies she was involved in hurricane relief tasks and, apart from major military exercises, she played a major part in the build-up of British forces in Sierra Leone in May 2000.

Above and below: *HMS Ocean (L12), the Royal Navy's latest and most important amphibious warfare vessel. (Royal Navy)*

HMS Ocean at anchor with stern loading ramp deployed.
(author)

SPECIFICATION

Type: LPH
Class: Ocean
Displacement: 21,758 tons full load
Length: 667.3ft (203.4m), flightdeck 557.7ft (170m)
Beam: 111.5ft (34m)
Draught: 21.3ft (6.6m)
Machinery: 2 Crossley Pielstick 16 PC2.6 V400 diesels, 23,900hp; 2 shafts, cp propellers; bow thruster
Speed & Range: 19kt; 9,200 miles (14,800km) at 15kt
Complement: 265 + 180 air group + troops
Missiles: nil
Guns: 3 Vulcan/Phalanx 20mm CIWS; 4 twin GAM-B03 20mm guns
ASW & USW: nil
Sensors: radar: Plessey Type 996 air and surface search; Kelvin Hughes Type 1007 navigation and aircraft control
Aircraft: 18 helicopters (max.)

LPD, Albion

HMS Albion **(L14). Artist's impression.**
(Royal Navy)

FOR DECADES BRITAIN'S AMPHIBIOUS warfare capability has relied on the two assault ships *Fearless* and *Intrepid*, which were built in the 1960s. Since that time they have been involved in numerous operations, including the Falklands War, and have proved their worth many times over. By the early 1990s it was apparent that they would need replacing, but it was not until 1996 that orders for two new ships, *Albion* and *Bulwark*, were placed with Vickers Shipbuilding and Engineering Ltd at Barrow in Furness (now part of BAE Systems). Subsequently, *Albion* was laid down in May 1998 and *Bulwark* some 12 months later, although neither will be completed until 2003 at the earliest, by which time *Fearless* will be almost 40 years old.

The Albion class ships will be larger than the ones they will replace, although the nominal troop capacity will be very similar. However, the accommodation standards and support services will be greatly superior, and the incorporation of a side ramp will make it much easier to embark troops, vehicles and supplies while alongside without the need for special port facilities. In addition, the ship's complement is reduced by about 200, making for considerable costs savings over the life of the ship. A large and well-equipped operations room, with comprehensive C² systems, will enable these ships to act as command vessels during amphibious operations. A total of three Merlin helicopters can be embarked, and a hangar is incorporated in the after-section of the large superstructure block, an improvement on the Fearless class, which had no hangar facilities. The flightdeck itself is sized to allow simultaneous operation of two helicopters, and can accept RAF Chinooks if required. The internal well deck can accommodate four LCU Mk.10s or four LCACs, while four LCVP Mk.5s are carried in davits amidships. The economical diesel electric machinery gives a speed of 18kt to conform with the LPH HMS *Ocean*.

HMS Fearless **is one of two older ships which will be replaced by the new Albion class LPDs. (author)**

SPECIFICATION

Type: LPD
Class: Albion
Displacement: 16,980 tons full load
Length: 577.4ft (176m)
Beam: 94.8ft (28.9m)
Draught: 21.7ft (6.6m)
Machinery: diesel electric; 2 Wärtsilä Vasa 16V 32E diesel generators, 17,000hp; 2 Wärtsilä Vasa 4R 32E diesel generators, 4,216hp; 2 motors, 2 shafts; bow thruster
Speed & Range: 18kt
Complement: 325 + troops
Missiles: nil
Guns: 2 Goalkeeper 30mm CIWS; 2 twin 20mm
ASW & USW: nil
Sensors: radar: Siemens Plessey 996 air and surface search; Racal Type 1008 navigation and aircraft control
Aircraft: 3 helicopters

LSD, Whidbey Island/Harpers Ferry

USS Whidbey Island (LSD-41).
(Guy Toremans)

USS Tortuga (LSD-46) with fleet oiler USNS
Patuxent (AO201).
(US Navy)

THIS SUBSTANTIAL BUILDING PROGRAMME goes back to 1981 when the lead ship, Whidbey Island (LSD-41), was laid down. She was subsequently completed in 1985 and was followed by a further seven ships, of which the last, Ashland (LSD-48) was commissioned in 1992.

The layout of these ships was based on the preceding Anchorage class ordered in the 1960s and features a large well deck, 440ft by 50ft (134m by 15m) and a variety of landing craft combinations can include four LCACs, 21 LCMs or 64 LVTs. A helicopter deck can accommodate two CH-53D Sea Stallion helicopters, although there are no hangar facilities. Two large cranes with 60 and 20-ton capacities respectively are fitted amidships. Up to 500 troops may be embarked with their vehicles and equipment, but the function of these ships is also to act as a provider of landing craft for other transports which do not carry their own.

Following on from the original eight ships, a further four were built as specialist cargo variants. Known as the Harpers Ferry class, these entered service between January 1995 and May 1998. The principal modification is the reduction in size of the well deck in order to provide more cargo capacity, but other changes include additional air conditioning, internal structural changes, repositioning of the defensive armament and the deletion of one of the cranes. Following successful trials aboard Whidbey Island, all 12 ships are being refitted with a new quick reaction combat system and ship self-defence system (QRCC/SSDS) which integrates the reactions of the RAM missile system and the Phalanx CIWS to give faster responses to threats. They will also receive ACDS to ensure operational compatibility with the Wasp, Tarawa and San Antonio class ships when forming as part of a co-ordinated amphibious warfare task force.

Whidbey Island class dock landing ship
USS Fort McHenry (LSD-43) with an LCAC
hovercraft running alongside.
(US Navy via USS Fort McHenry)

SPECIFICATION

Type: LSD
Class: Whidbey Island/Harpers Ferry
Displacement: 11,125 tons light, 15,725 tons (Whidbey Island) or 16,750 tons (Harpers Ferry) full load
Length: 609.5ft (185.8m)
Beam: 84ft (25.6m)
Draught: 20.5ft (6.3m)
Machinery: 4 Colt SEMT-Pielstick 16 PC2.5 V400 diesels, 40,000hp (max.); 2 shafts, cp propellers
Speed & Range: 22kt; 9,200 miles (14,800km) at 18kt
Complement: 340 + troops
Missiles: 1 or 2 Mk.49 launchers, RAM short-range SAM
Guns: 2 Vulcan/Phalanx 20mm CIWS, 2 25mm, 8 12.7mm (0.5in) machine-guns
ASW & USW: SLQ-25 Nixie decoy
Sensors: radar: Decca 1226 navigation
Aircraft: helicopter platform

LPD, Rotterdam/Galicia

The Spanish LPD Galicia (L51). (Bazán)

The Rotterdam (L800) was commissioned in 1988. Note the Goalkeeper CIWS on the foredeck. (Schelde Shipbuilding)

THE ORIGIN OF THIS VESSEL dates from the mid-1980s, the final design being drawn up following a feasibility study in 1988. Originally conceived as a national programme, it became an international project in 1991 when the Spanish Navy took an interest in the design and common staff requirements were adopted. The *Rotterdam* was laid down in 1996, launched in 1997 and commissioned on 18 April 1998; a second Netherlands ship is projected to enter service around 2007. In the meantime, two Spanish ships, *Galicia* and *Castilla*, were laid down in the Bazán yard at Ferrol, and these entered service in 1998 and 2000 respectively.

The Spanish ships differ in detail from the Netherlands vessels principally in that they have a direct diesel propulsion system employing two Caterpillar 3612 diesels for a total of 12,500hp, and the indigenous Meroka CIWS replaces the Goalkeeper system. The Dutch ships are configured to carry a marine battalion of 611 men complete with all their arms and support equipment, including tanks and AFVs. There are docking facilities below the after-section of the flightdeck for four LCU/LCMs or six LCVPs. The hangar can accommodate up to six NH-90 or four EHI Merlin helicopters, although only two at a time can operate from the flightdeck. While giving the Dutch (and Spanish) Navy a substantial boost to their amphibious capability, the *Rotterdam* is designed to perform a number of other roles if required. These include acting as a platform for anti-submarine helicopters, transporting army and air force equipment, support platform for MCMVs, and supporting humanitarian and disaster relief operations.

The *Rotterdam* was built by Schelde Shipbuilding using a modular construction system, and based on this experience the company is now offering its Enforcer design, which offers a range of LPDs displacing between 9,000 and 14,000 tons by various combinations of standard modules, each of which can be customised.

SPECIFICATION

Type: LPD
Class: Rotterdam
Displacement: 12,720 tons full load
Length: 544.6ft (183.7m)
Beam: 82ft (25m)
Draught: 19.3ft (5.9m)
Machinery: diesel electric; 4 Stok-Wärtsilä 12SW28 diesel generators, 14.6MW; 2 Holec motors, 16,320hp; 2 shafts plus a bow thruster
Speed & Range: 19kt; 6,000 miles (9,650km) at 12kt
Complement: 113 + 611 troops
Missiles: nil
Guns: 2 30mm (1.18in) Goalkeeper CIWS; 4 Oerlikon 20mm
ASW & USW: SLQ-25 Nixie torpedo decoy system
Sensors: radar: Signaal DA08 air and surface search; Signal Scout surface search; navigation and aircraft control
Aircraft: 4 or 6 helicopters

LSD, Foudre

THE FRENCH NAVY OPERATES TWO FOUDRE class landing platform dock ships, *Foudre* (L9011) and *Siroco* (L9012), which were commissioned in 1990 and 1998. The ships were built at the Brest Naval Dockyard of DCN and are currently assigned to the *Force d'Action Navale* based at the Toulon Mediterranean Command.

The Foudre class is capable of landing and supporting a mechanised armoured regiment of the French rapid deployment force, and other missions include mobile logistic support for naval forces and humanitarian missions. These ships have a 460,000 cu. ft (13,000 cu. m) well dock which can be used as a floating dock or to carry land vehicles. The well dock can accommodate either 10 medium-size landing craft (LCMs) or one mechanised landing craft (LSM) and four medium-sized landing craft (LCMs). Mobile decks can be used to provide vehicle parking space so that up to 200 vehicles could be transported if the landing craft are not required. The cargo lift has a 52-ton capacity and the 39 ft (12m) crane is rated to carry 37 tons of cargo.

The ship's complement is 210 crew with 13 officers, and in addition it can accommodate 467 passengers or troops. With 700 crew and passengers, the ship has an endurance of 30 days. In times of crisis the ship can accommodate up to 1,600 people. To meet military and humanitarian requirements, Foudre class ships provide hospital facilities for large-scale medical and evacuation missions, including two fully equipped operating theatres and 47 beds.

The ship, which has a 15,600 sq. ft (1,450 sq. m) flightdeck, can accommodate up to seven Super Puma helicopters. There are three helicopter landing spots, two on the flightdeck and one on the 4,300 sq. ft (400 sq. m) deck well rolling cover. The flightdeck is equipped with a SAMAHE haul down system, and a double hangar incorporated in the forward superstructure has capacity for two Super Frelon helicopters or up to four Super Puma helicopters. The Foudre class ships are equipped with DCN's SENIT 8 combat data system and an OPSMER command support system, while the communication suite is integrated with the Syracuse satellite communications system.

Above and above left: Foudre *(L9011)*, landing ship dock (LSD). (Marine Nationale, *France*)

SPECIFICATION

Type: LSD
Class: Foudre
Displacement: 8,190 tons standard, 12,400 tons full load
Length: 551ft (168m)
Beam: 77.1ft (23.5m)
Draught: 17ft (5.2m)
Machinery: 2 SEMT-Pielstick 16 PC2.5 V400 diesels, 20,800hp; 2 shafts, cp propellers; bow thruster
Speed & Range: 21kt; 11,000 miles (17,700km) at 15kt
Complement: 223 + troops
Missiles: 2 lightweight Simbad twin launchers, Matra Mistral short-range SAM
Guns: 1 Bofors 40mm, 2 Giat 20mm and 2 12.7mm (0.5in) machine-guns
ASW & USW: nil
Sensors: radar: DRBV 21A air and surface search; Racal Decca 2459 surface search; RM1229 navigation
Aircraft: 2 or 4 helicopters

LPD, Osumi

Osumi *(LST 4001). The first of two helicopter-capable LSTs for the JMSDF. (RAN)*

THIS CLASS HAD ITS ORIGINS in a projected 5,500-ton LST dating back to the late 1980s. However, this was not approved and it was subsequently recast as an LPD incorporating a flightdeck and stern well deck. The *Osumi* was finally ordered in 1993 and laid down in December 1995, launched in November 1996 and commissioned on 11 March 1998. Work began on a second vessel in late 1999, and this is due for completion in 2002 while a third ship has been ordered for delivery in 2003.

Officially a troop carrier and assault ship with a stern dock, the *Osumi* can carry 330 troops and 10 tanks which can be carried ashore aboard two LCACs carried in the stern well dock. Also, two large CH-47J helicopters can operate simultaneously from landing spots at the after end of the flightdeck, while there is additional flightdeck space for parking more helicopters forward of the island. A side ramp on the starboard side, forward of the island, allows for easy embarkation of stores and vehicles while alongside.

Despite its small size and relatively limited capabilities, this ship represents an important step forward for the JMSDF, which has been limited in its operations by political restrictions. In particular, aircraft carriers are seen as being offensive weapons and consequently great emphasis is placed on the very limited nature of the aviation facilities of these LPDs. Nevertheless, the Osumi class now allows Japan to carry out military operations well outside domestic waters, and they could easily be developed to allow the operation of fixed-wing VSTOL aircraft in the future, although the existing very wide superstructure island amidships at present takes up too much deck space.

Osumi *underway showing clear run of helicopter flightdeck. (JMSDF)*

SPECIFICATION

Type: LPD
Class: Osumi
Displacement: 8,900 tons standard
Length: 584ft (178m)
Beam: 84.6ft (25.8m)
Draught: 19.7ft (6m)
Machinery: 2 Mitsui 16V42MA diesels, 27,600hp; 2 shafts; bow thrusters
Speed & Range: 22kt
Complement: 135 + troops
Missiles: nil
Guns: 2 Vulcan/Phalanx 6-barrelled 20mm CIWS
ASW & USW: nil
Sensors: radar: OPS-14C air search; OPS-28D surface search; OPS-20 navigation
Aircraft: 2 helicopters

LPD, San Giorgio

THE THREE SAN GIORGIO CLASS amphibious transport dock ships in service with the Italian Navy were built by Fincantieri at its Riva Trigoso shipyard and comprise MM *San Giorgio* (L9892), commissioned in 1987, MM *San Marco* (L9893), commissioned in 1988, and MM *San Giusto* (L9894), commissioned in 1994. All three are based at Brindisi on Italy's Adriatic coast.

The San Giorgio class ships can lift a battalion of troops, with up to 30 medium tanks or 36 tracked armoured vehicles. The stern floodable dock can accommodate three LCM (or MTM) landing craft each capable of transporting 30 tons of materiel. Three davits on the main deck are provided for the deployment of three LCVP (or MTP) landing craft and a patrol boat. A 30-ton lift and a two-hook travelling crane, each hook rated to carry 40 tons, are installed on the ship providing the capability of autonomous loading and unloading operations completely independent of harbour facilities. The flightdeck was designed to support operations by either three SH-3D Sea King or five AB 212 helicopters, although there are no hangar facilities.

Although all are manned as naval vessels, the third ship (*San Giusto*, launched in 1993) was actually paid for by the Ministry of Civil Protection and is available at short notice for disaster relief tasks and has hospital facilities for peacetime rescue and humanitarian operations. As completed, she had a full load displacement 300 tons higher than her sister ships and no bow doors for beach landings. The three davits for the deployment of landing craft and the patrol boat were relocated to a sponson installed on the port side of the ship instead of on the flightdeck, and these modifications will be applied to the two earlier ships in refits commencing in 2000 in order to allow two EH101 helicopters and two medium helicopters (NH-90 or AB 212) to operate simultaneously.

A planned 22,500-ton LHA has now evolved into a fully capable aircraft carrier which will commission in 2007.

San Giorgio (L9892), the first of three LPDs built for the Italian Navy and completed in 1987. (Marina Militare, Italy)

San Giusto (L9894). Note enlarged island and portside sponson to accommodate three LCVPs. (Marina Militare, Italy)

SPECIFICATION

Type: LPD
Class: San Giorgio
Displacement: 6,687 tons standard, 7,665 tons full load
Length: 437.2ft (133.3m)
Beam: 67.3ft (20.5m)
Draught: 17.4ft 5.3m)
Machinery: 2 Fincantieri GMT A420.12 diesels, 16,800hp; 2 shafts, cp propellers; bow thruster
Speed & Range: 21kt; 7,500 miles (12,070km) at 16kt
Complement: 163 + troops
Missiles: nil
Guns: 1 OTO Melera 3in (76mm)/62 automatic gun; 2 single 25mm; 2 12.7mm (0.5in) machine-guns
ASW & USW: nil
Sensors: radar: SMA SPS-702 surface search; SMA SPN-748 navigation; SPG-70 fire control
Aircraft: up to 5 helicopters

LST, Ropucha (Type 775)

Ropucha class Type 775 LST at speed.
(RAF Kinloss/MoD)

HISTORICALLY, RUSSIAN FORCES have always operated on internal lines of communication and consequently have not been required to deploy large amphibious expeditionary forces such as those deployed by the British and US navies in World War II. Their current amphibious capability is built around a fleet of LSTs and a single operational LPD.

The backbone of the Russian amphibious warfare fleet is the Type 775 Ropucha, all of which were built in Polish shipyards. Some 24 of the original Ropucha I were built in two batches of 12, the first group being completed between 1974 and 1978, and the second in 1980 to 1988. These were followed by three Ropucha IIs (Type 775M) completed 1990 to 1992, and this version differed mainly in having an upgraded defensive armament and improved radar outfit. Troop capacity is the same in both versions, and although exact combinations can vary, a typical load would be 10 MBTs and 190 soldiers. The tank deck runs the whole length of the ship using the ro-ro principle with integral bow and stern ramps. As with other components of the Russian fleet, amphibious forces have been drastically reduced in recent years and probably fewer than a dozen Ropuchas are currently operational.

A follow-on to these LSTs was the Type 1174 Ivan Rogov class LPD of which three ships were completed by 1991, although a fourth ship cancelled before completion. At 14,000 tons full load, these were substantially larger than the Ropucha class and could operate up to four Kamov Ka-29 helicopters from a stern flightdeck and a landing spot on the foredeck. They could carry up to 20 tanks and 550 troops. A stern well deck could contain six LCMs or three air-cushion vehicles but, unlike western LPDs, a bow ramp for offloading tanks and vehicles was also provided. Only one ship of this class (*Mitrofan Moskalenko*) remains in service.

With most Russian amphibious operations likely to occur in shallow waters such as the Baltic or Black seas, considerable effort was put into developing large air-cushion vehicles and experimental wings in ground effect (WIG) craft, but very few of these have been retained.

SPECIFICATION

Type: LST
Class: Ropucha (Type 775)
Displacement: 4,400 tons full load
Length: 369.1ft (112.5m)
Beam: 49.2ft (15m)
Draught: 12.1ft (3.7m)
Machinery: 2 Zgoda Sulzer 16ZVB40/48 diesels, 19,230hp; 2 shafts
Speed & Range: 17.5kt; 6,000 miles (9,650km) at 12kt
Complement: 95 + troops
Missiles: up to 4 quadruple launchers, SA-N-5 Grail short-range SAM (some ships only)
Guns: 2 twin 57mm (2.2in)/80 (Ropucha I) or 1 76mm (3in)/60 automatic (Ropucha II); 1 AK630 6-barrelled 30mm CIWS (Ropucha II)
ASW & USW: nil
Sensors: radar: Strut Curve or Cross Dome (Ropucha II) air and surface search; Don 2 or Nayada navigation; Muff Cob or Bass Tilt fire control; sonar: Mouse Tail VDS in some ships
Aircraft: nil

LOGISTIC SUPPORT VESSELS

IT WAS THE US NAVY WHICH, in World War II, perfected a system of keeping a fleet at sea for long periods by replenishing stocks of fuel, ammunition and other supplies from a highly organised fleet train. Today the support of ships at sea is a very specialised affair and all major navies deploy a variety of logistic support ships. Many of these are very large and can provide a 'one-stop' service to transfer both fuel and stores in a relatively short time using complex handling gear for transfer between ships underway, and, in some cases, also carry their own helicopters for vertical replenishment (Vertrep) tasks. A typical example is the Fort Victoria class of fleet replenishment ships which, in terms of displacement, are the largest ships operated by the Royal Navy.

AOE, Supply

USS **Bridge** *(AOE-10), Supply class fast combat support ship. (US Navy)*

KNOWN AS FAST COMBAT SUPPORT SHIPS, the Supply class design is based on the earlier Sacramento class which was built between 1961 and 1970. The main difference is the use of gas turbines for propulsion instead of conventional steam turbines. The lead ship, USS *Supply*, was laid down in 1989 and completed in February 1994, and two more (*Rainier, Arctic*) were commissioned in 1995. The fourth and last ship (*Bridge*) entered service in 1998. All four were built for the US Navy by National Steel and Shipbuilding of San Diego.

These vessels are designed to accompany carrier task forces for which their relatively high speed and long range are essential assets. The ships are fitted with state-of-the-art replenishment at sea (RAS) equipment to handle the enormous spectrum of fuel and stores carried on board. For example, the liquid cargo stowage includes 156,000 barrels of fuel (e.g. Avcat military kerosene gas-turbine fuel), 500 55-gallon barrels of lubrication oil and 20,000 gallons of cargo water together with a cargo fuel control system. The dry cargo stowage includes cargo ordnance holds for 1,800 tons of ammunition, a 400-ton refrigerated cargo hold, 250 tons of general cargo and 800 bottles of bottled gas. Additionally, there is special cargo accommodation for oversize items such as cable reels and containerised jet engines. To handle this there is a comprehensive cargo transfer system with a dedicated cargo control centre. There are five fuel at sea (FAS) stations, six replenishment

at sea (RAS) stations, four 10-ton cargo booms, and a vertical replenishment position for simultaneous use by two helicopters. Normally, three US Navy UH-46E Sea Knight helicopters are embarked and are housed in the triple hangar opening onto the stern flightdeck.

SPECIFICATION

Type: AOE
Class: Supply
Displacement: 19,700 tons light, 49,000 tons full load
Length: 753.7ft (229.7m)
Beam: 107ft (32.6m)
Draught: 38ft (11.6m)
Machinery: 4 LM2500 gas turbines, 105,000hp; 2 shafts
Speed & Range: 25kt; 6,000 miles (9,650km) at 22kt
Complement: 531
Missiles: 1 Mk.29 octuple launcher, Sea Sparrow short-range SAM
Guns: 2 Vulcan/Phalanx 6-barrelled 20mm CIWS; 2 single 25mm; 4 12.7mm (0.5in) machine-guns
ASW & USW: SLQ-25 Nixie torpedo decoy
Sensors: radar: Mk.23 TAS air search; SPS-67 air and surface search; SPS-64 navigation; Mk.95 fire control
Aircraft: 3 UH-46E Sea Knight helicopters

AOR, Fort Victoria

RFA Fort Victoria *(A387).*
(Royal Navy)

AN AMBITIOUS PLAN TO BUILD SIX of these large fleet replenishments ships was not implemented and only two were completed. The first of these, RFA *Fort Victoria* (A387), was laid down by Harland & Wolff at its Belfast yard on 4 April 1988. She was launched on 12 June 1990 and commissioned on 24 June 1994 after a final fitting out by Cammell Laird at Liverpool. Her sister ship, *Fort George* (A388), was built at Swan Hunter's yard on the River Tyne and was laid down on 9 March 1989, launched on 1 March 1991 and commissioned on 16 July 1993.

The primary role of the Royal Fleet Auxiliary (RFA), a flotilla of 22 ships manned by civilians and owned by the Ministry of Defence, is to supply the Royal Navy at sea. The RFA also provides the Royal Navy with seaborne aviation training facilities in addition to secure logistical support and amphibious operations capability for the Royal Marines and the British Army. RFA *Fort Victoria* and *Fort George* combine the functions of fleet support tanker and stores support ship. They have the capacity to carry a cargo of up to 220,850 cu. ft (6,250 cu. m) of solids stores plus 441,700 cu. ft (12,500 cu. m) of liquids. The four dual-purpose replenishment rigs fitted amidships enable RFA *Fort Victoria* to replenish two warships with both fuel and stores simultaneously.

Fuel transfer is accomplished by suspending a hose from a tensioned cable, the jackstay, which runs from the RFA to the receiving warship. The hose is fitted with a quick-coupling probe to mate with the receiving point on the warship. Once the hose has been connected, fuel is pumped across to the receiving ship. During a stores transfer the jackstay supports a 'traveller', a travelling hoist, to which loads of up to two tons may be coupled. As well as the main replenishment rigs, RFA *Victoria* is also fitted with an additional refuelling rig, called a Hudson Reel, at the stern. Stern refuelling is not as efficient as beam replenishment but it is safer in severe weather conditions.

These ships are also fitted with a two-spot flightdeck, a hangar and maintenance facilities for five Sea King-sized helicopters. This gives the ship an enhanced capability to re-supply warships in a task group by vertical replenishment (Vertrep). The flightdecks are also capable of providing an emergency landing facility for the Royal Navy's Sea Harrier.

RFA Fort George *(A388).*
(author)

SPECIFICATION

Type: AOR
Class: Fort Victoria
Displacement: 36,850 tons full load
Length: 667.7ft (203.5m)
Beam: 99.7ft (30.4m)
Draught: 32ft (9.8m)
Machinery: 2 Crossley SEMT-Pielstick 16 PC2.6 V400 diesels, 23,904hp; 2 shafts
Speed & Range: 20kt
Complement: 134 + up to 154 air group
Missiles: nil
Guns: 2 Vulcan/Phalanx 6-barrelled 20mm CIWS; 2 single DS30B 30mm
ASW & USW: Type 182 towed decoy
Sensors: radar: Type 996 air search; Type 1007 navigation; NUCLEAS aircraft control
Aircraft: up to 5 helicopters

UNITED KINGDOM
ATS, Argus

IN ADDITION TO VARIOUS LOGISTIC SUPPORT vessels intended to accompany warships at sea, there is a whole range of other types engaged on an infinite variety of tasks essential to the operation of a modern navy. These include tankers, transports, water carriers, dockyard craft, mooring vessels and survey craft, to name but a few. Training is a vital function, and while some navies employ specially designed ships such as the French *Jeanne d'Arc*, others use converted or modified naval or mercantile vessels. Coming into the latter category is the Royal Navy's aviation training ship (ATS) RFA *Argus* which was originally completed as the ro-ro container ship *Contender Bezant* by CNR Breda of Venice, Italy.

During the Falklands War in 1982 a number of merchant ships had been converted to carry and operate helicopters, and the success of this concept, despite the tragic sinking of the *Atlantic Conveyor* with a precious cargo of Chinook helicopters, prompted the decision to carry out a more extensive conversion of suitable vessels. Accordingly, the *Contender Bezant* was purchased in 1984 and underwent a four-year rebuild at Harland & Wolff, Belfast, recommissioning in June 1988 as RFA *Argus*. The conversion entailed the construction of a long flightdeck aft of the forward superstructure and the previous vehicle deck became a hangar which is served by two lifts. As converted, her primary role was as a helicopter training vessel and she replaced the smaller RFA *Engadine*, which had been built in the 1960s and was too small to support sustained operations by larger helicopters such as the Sea King and the then projected EH101 Merlin.

However, *Argus* was also fitted with an automated combat information system enabling her to take part in military operations if required, and in the 1991 Gulf War she was deployed as a casualty-receiving and hospital ship, and in the later Adriatic operations in support of UN forces in Bosnia she acted as a temporary LPH. However, her limited accommodation was a serious drawback in this role and, in any case, her withdrawal from the normal training role caused severe problems at home. Despite this she was called on to support British forces in Sierra Leone in late 2000 after fire aboard the LPD *Fearless*.

Another secondary task is to act as an aircraft transport, and for this purpose she can carry 12 Sea Harriers, although flight operations are not possible.

Above and below: RFA Argus *(A135), an aviation support ship converted from a mercantile container vessel. (author)*

SPECIFICATION

Type: ATS
Class: Argus
Displacement: 18,280 tons standard, 26,420 tons full load
Length: 574.5ft (175.1m)
Beam: 99.7ft (30.4m)
Draught: 27ft (8.2m)
Machinery: 2 Lindholmen SEMT-Pielstick 18 PC2.5 V400 diesels, 23,400 hp; 2 shafts
Speed & Range: 23,000 miles (37,000km) at 19kt
Complement: 80 (ship), 252 (total)
Missiles: nil
Guns: 2 twin 30mm, 4 single 12.7mm (0.5in) machine-guns
ASW & USW: Type 182 torpedo decoy
Sensors: radar: Type 994 air search; Type 1006 short-range air and surface
Aircraft: 6 helicopters

AOR, Durance

FIVE OF THESE REPLENISHMENT tankers were built for the French Navy between 1973 and 1990 (*Durance*, *Meuse*, *Var*, *Marne*, *Somme*). Four of these remain in service but the lead ship, *Durance* was sold to Argentina in 1999. The last three vessels (*Var*, *Marne*, *Somme*) were completed with greatly extended forward superstructures providing additional accommodation and operational spaces which enable them to be used as command ships.

In this form, at least one is normally deployed to the Indian or Pacific oceans to act as a flagship for French forces in the area. A small military force of marines is embarked and two LCVPs are carried to transport them ashore. A hangar installed between the twin funnels can accommodate a single light helicopter (Lynx, Dauphin or Alouette III) but the flightdeck is capable of accepting larger helicopters such as the Super Frelon. The cargo capacity of these ships varies, but *Var* and *Marne* carry 5,090 tons of fuel oil, 3,310 tons of diesel oil, 1,090 tons of JP-5 aviation fuel, 260 tons of distilled water, 170 tons of ammunition, 180 tons of provisions and 45 tons of spare parts and general stores.

In addition to the French vessels, a further Durance class AOR was built at Cockatoo Dockyards, Sydney, for the RAN and commissioned as HMAS *Success* in 1986. Defensive armament includes two Vulcan/Phalanx CIWS and the hangar is modified to accept helicopters up to Sea King size. Two modified Durance class ships were also built in Marseilles for Saudi Arabia and delivered in 1983 and 1984. These

Marne (A630), Durance class AOR entering Plymouth. (D. Hannaford)

were shortened by approximately 70ft (22m) and the second fuelling gantry deleted, but were in most other respects virtually identical to the original design.

SPECIFICATION

Type: AOR
Class: Durance
Displacement: 17,900 tons full load
Length: 515.9ft (157.3m)
Beam: 69.5ft (21.2m)
Draught: 38.5ft (10.8m)
Machinery: 2 SEMT-Pielstick 16 PC2.5 V400 diesels, 20,800hp; 2 shafts, cp propellers
Speed & Range: 19kt; 9,000 miles (14,480km) at 15kt
Complement: 164
Missiles: 2 Simbad twin launchers, Mistral very-short-range SAM
Guns: 3 single 30mm; 4 12.7mm (0.5in) machine-guns
ASW & USW: nil
Sensors: Racal Decca 1226 navigation and aircraft control
Aircraft: 1 helicopter

AOR, Amsterdam/Patiño

Patiño *(A14), Spanish-built version of the Amsterdam class AOR.*
(Bazán)

THIS FAST COMBAT SUPPORT SHIP was laid down in 1992 and completed in September 1995 when it replaced one of the two Poolster class AORs which were built in the 1970s. A second Amsterdam class ship is expected to be ordered to enter service in 2006 when the remaining Poolster will be retired.

The design features two standard RAS stations on either beam and cargo capacity includes 6,815 tons of diesel, 1,660 tons of aviation fuel and 290 tons of stores and provisions. The stern flightdeck is served by a large hangar which can accommodate three small/medium helicopters such as the Lynx, SH-3D Sea King or NH-90, or alternatively two large EH101 helicopters could be carried, although at present the Dutch Navy has no plans to acquire such aircraft.

The design of the *Amsterdam* was the result of close co-operation between The Netherlands and Spain, and a sister ship was built by Bazán at Ferrol and delivered to the Spanish Navy in June 1995. This ship, *Patiño*, differs only in detail from the *Amsterdam* and for defensive purposes carries the Spanish design Meroka CIWS atop the hangar instead of the Goalkeeper fitted to the Dutch ship. *Patiño* is specifically tasked as a carrier group support ship, working with the *Príncipe de Asturias* and her escorts. Spain also operates a smaller AOR, *Marqués de la Ensenada*, which displaces 13,500 tons at full load and was completed in 1991. There are two RAS stations, one on either beam, and a single Sea King helicopter can operate from the after flightdeck in the Vertrep role, but there is no hangar.

Amsterdam *(A836), fast combat support ship of the Netherlands Navy. (Schelde Shipbuilding)*

SPECIFICATION

Type: AOR
Class: Amsterdam
Displacement: 6,000 tons light, 17,040 tons full load
Length: 544.6ft (166m)
Beam: 72.2ft (22m)
Draught: 26.2ft (8m)
Machinery: 2 Bazán/Burmeister & Wain 16V 40/45 diesels, 24,000hp; 1 shaft, cp propeller
Speed & Range: 20kt; 13,440 miles (21,625km) at 20kt
Complement: 160 + air group
Missiles: nil
Guns: 1 Goalkeeper 30mm CIWS; 2 single Oerlikon 20mm
ASW & USW: SLQ-25 Nixie towed decoy
Sensors: radar: F-band surface search and aircraft control
Aircraft: 3 helicopters

AOR, Etna

THIS IS ITALY'S LARGEST AND NEWEST AOR and was originally ordered in July 1994. Built by Fincantieri at Riva Trigoso, she was laid down in July 1995, launched on 12 July 1997 and commissioned on 29 August 1998.

As completed, the 3in (76mm) gun was not fitted and, although the design provides for the installation of a CIWS, this also was not included. The stern flightdeck and hangar are sized to accommodate either an SH-3D Sea King or EH101 Merlin helicopter. Alternatively, two smaller Agusta Bell AB 212s may be carried. There are two RAS stations on either beam for underway replenishment and transfer of solid and liquid cargo, including oil fuel, aviation fuel and fresh water. The maximum rate of diesel fuel transfer is 650 tons per hour and the ship is also fitted with a stern refuelling station which can be used when the sea state precludes the use of the beam stations. The cargo capacity includes 4,700 tons of diesel fuel (5,400 tons overload), 1,200 tons of aviation fuel, and 160 tons of fresh water, as well as space for up to 12 standard storage containers. There are three reverse osmosis desalination plants for the production of fresh water, each at a rate of 40 tons per day. The ship has two 50-ton cranes and two 4-ton lifts.

The *Etna*'s main role is to support the long-range missions of a naval squadron, which would typically include an aircraft carrier and its escorts, but she is also capable of providing assistance and support in humanitarian and disaster relief operations. In such scenarios the ship can provide electrical power, fresh water and prepared meals, and also has fully equipped hospital and medical facilities on board.

The *Etna* supplements two Stromboli class replenishment tankers which were commissioned in

Etna (A5326), replenishment tanker (AOR) completed for the Marina Militare in 1998. (Marina Militare, Italy)

1975 and 1978. At 8,700 tons full load these are much smaller than the newer ship. In recent years the Italian Navy has taken part in several major deployments outside its traditional Mediterranean theatre of operations and consequently there was a need for a larger AOR such as the Etna class. This was particularly important with the commissioning of the aircraft carrier *Giuseppe Garibaldi* in the 1980s.

SPECIFICATION

Type: AOR
Class: Etna
Displacement: 13,400 tons full load
Length: 480.6ft (91.9m)
Beam: 68.9ft (21m)
Draught: 24.3ft (7.4m)
Machinery: 2 Sulzer 12 ZAV 40S diesels, 22,400hp; 2 shafts; bow thruster
Speed & Range: 21kt; 8,760 miles (14,100km) at 18kt
Complement: 160
Missiles: nil
Guns: 1 OTO Melera 3in (76mm)/62 automatic; 2 25mm guns
ASW & USW: nil
Sensors: radar: SPS-702 I-band surface search; SPN-753 navigation
Aircraft: 1 or 2 helicopters

AOR, Endeavour

HMNZS Endeavour (A11).
(Guy Toremans)

NOT EVERY NAVY CAN AFFORD large and sophisticated auxiliaries and a common solution is to adapt a mercantile hull or design. Typical of this method is HMNZS *Endeavour*, which was built for New Zealand by Hyundai, South Korea. Laid down on 10 April 1987, she was launched on 14 August 1987 and commissioned on 8 April 1988. By Western standards, the 12-month period from laying down to completion would seem to be very efficient and it is, therefore, surprising to learn that completion was actually delayed by various factors including labour troubles at the shipyard and late delivery of the propulsion machinery!

Basically, the ship is a straightforward commercial tanker, modified by the fitting of two beam RAS stations amidships, and a trailing stern rig. A total of 7,500 tons of diesel is available for transfer, as well as 100 tons of Avcat, while 20 containers can be stowed on deck in front of the bridge. A flightdeck and hangar (offset to starboard) are situated at the stern and a single Kaman Seasprite helicopter can be accommodated if required, although this is not always embarked as these are normally deployed aboard the RNZN frigates. Built and operated to mercantile standards, the crew complement is relatively small by naval standards and this is achieved by automation wherever possible. For example, the main and auxiliary machinery spaces are normally unmanned except for routine maintenance periods. A satellite communication system is fitted.

SPECIFICATION

Type: AOR
Class: Endeavour
Displacement: 12,390 tons full load
Length: 453.1ft (138.1m)
Beam: 60ft (18.4m)
Draught: 23ft (7.3m)
Machinery: 1 MAN-Burmeister & Wain 12V32/36 diesel, 5,780hp; 1 shaft, cp propeller
Speed & Range: 9,200 miles (14,800km) at 13.5kt
Complement: 49
Missiles: nil
Guns: nil
ASW & USW: nil
Sensors: radar: Racal 1290A/9 navigation; ARPA 16S90S, I-band
Aircraft: 1 helicopter

Glossary

AAW	Anti Air Warfare
ACDS	Advanced Combat Direction System
AEW	Airborne Early Warning
AIP	Air Independent Propulsion. A closed-cycle propulsion system for submarines.
A/S	Anti-Submarine
ASROC	Anti-Submarine Rocket. An American-developed ship-launched missile carrying an anti-submarine homing torpedo.
ASW	Anti-Submarine Warfare
C²	Command and Communications
C³	Command, Communications and Control
CIWS	Close In Weapons System. A very short-range automated weapons system, usually gun-based, intended primarily as a last-ditch defence against anti-ship missiles.
CODAD	Combined Diesel AND Diesel. A propulsion system in which the ship may be driven by any combination of several diesel engines.
CODAG	Combined Diesel AND Gas Turbine. A propulsion system in which the ship may be driven by either gas turbines or diesel engines, or a combination of both.
CODLAG	Combined Diesel Electric AND Gas Turbine. A propulsion system in which the ship may be driven by either gas turbines or electric motors powered by diesel generators.
CODOG	Combined Diesel OR Gas Turbine. A propulsion system in which the ship may be driven by gas turbines or diesel engines.
COGAG	Combined Gas Turbine AND Gas Turbine. A propulsion system in which the ship may be driven by combinations of units from one or both of two sets of gas turbines.
COGOG	Combined Gas Turbine OR Gas Turbine. A propulsion system in which the ship may be driven by combinations of units from one of two sets of gas turbines, but not both.
CONAS	Combined Nuclear AND Steam Turbine. A propulsion system in which steam turbines are driven by steam produced by either conventional boilers or a nuclear powerplant.
cp	controllable pitch
ERGM	Extended-Range Guided Munition
FNS	French Naval Ship
ft	feet (unit of measurement)
GRP	Glassfibre Reinforced Products
HE	High Explosive
HMAS	Her Majesty's Australian Ship
HMCS	Her Majesty's Canadian Ship
HMS	Her Majesty's Ship
hp	horsepower
INS	Indian Navy Ship
IR	Infra Red
JMSDF	Japanese Maritime Self-Defence Force
kt	knot
LAMPS	Light Airborne Multi-Purpose System (helicopter)
m	metre (unit of measurement)
MBT	Main Battle Tank
MCM	Mine Countermeasures
MG	machine-gun
MIRV	Multiple Independently Targeted Re-entry Vehicles
mm	millimetre (unit of measurement)
MW	megawatt (unit of electrical power)
NGS	Naval Gunfire Support
oa	overall
PDMS	Point Defence Missile System
PLAN	People's Liberation Army Navy (China)
pp	between perpendiculars
PWR	Pressurised Water Reactor
RAM	Rolling Airframe Missile. A NATO-developed short-range highly manoeuvrable SAM.
RAN	Royal Australian Navy
RAS	Replenishment At Sea
RFA	Royal Fleet Auxiliary
RN	Royal Navy (United Kingdom)
RNZN	Royal New Zealand Navy
ROV	Remote Operated Vehicle
RPV	Remotely Piloted Vehicle
SAM	Surface-to-Air Missile
SATCOM	Satellite Communications
SLBM	Submarine-Launched Ballistic Missile
SLCM	Submarine-Launched Cruise Missile
SSM	Surface-to-Surface Missile
STOVL	Short Take-Off, Vertical Landing
STWS	Ships Torpedo Weapon System
TAS	Towed Array Sonar
TBMD	Theatre Ballistic Missile Defence
TLAM	Tomahawk Land Attack Missile
TIR	Target Indicating Radar
UAE	United Arab Emirates
UN	United Nations
US	United States
USN	United States Navy
USS	United States Ship
VDS	Variable Depth Sonar
Vertrep	Vertical Replenishment – stores transfer between ships by helicopter.

Index

Destroyers and Frigates

Name	Type	Country	No.
ANZAC	FFG	Australia/ New Zealand	75
Arleigh Burke	DDG	United States	50
Asagiri	DDG	Japan	71
Brandenburg (Type 123)	FFG	Germany	65
Bremen (Type 122)	FFG	Germany	76
Cassard (Type F70)	DDG	France	63
De La Penne	DDG	Italy	62
Delhi	DDG	India	52
De Zeven Provincien	DDG	Netherlands	57
Duke (Type 23)	FFG	United Kingdom	70
F100 Alvaro de Bazán	DDG	Spain	58
Floreal	FFG	France	85
Georges Leygues (Type F70)	DDG	France	67
Godavari	FFG	India	73
Halifax	FFH	Canada	66
Iroquois	DDG	Canada	60
Jiangwei (Type 053 H2G)	FFG	China	86
Karel Doorman (M Class)	FFG	Netherlands	80
Kongo	DDG	Japan	51
Kortenaer/ van Heemskerck	FFG	Netherlands	78
Krivak (Type 1135)	FFG	Russia	77
La Fayette	FFG	France	74
Lekiu	FFG	Malaysia (UK)	87
Luhu	DDG	China	69
Maestrale/Lupo	FFG	Italy	84
MEKO 200	FFG	Greece/Portugal/ Turkey	82
MEKO 360	DDG/FFG	Argentina/Nigeria	81
Murasame	DDG	Japan	61
Okpo	DDG	South Korea	72
Oliver Hazard Perry	FFG	United States	83
Sachsen (Type 124)	FFG	Germany	59
Shirane/Haruna	DDG	Japan	56
Sovremenny (Type 956)	DDG	Russia	55
Spruance	DDG	United States	54
Thetis	FF	Denmark	79
Type 22	FFG	United Kingdom	64
Type 42	DG	United Kingdom	68
Udaloy	FFG	Russia	53

Small Warships

Name	Type	Country	No.
Avenger	MCM	United States	91
Barzan (Vita)	PCFG	Qatar (UK)	104
Eilat (Saar 5)	FSG	Israel	93
Éridan (Tripartite)	MHC	France/Belgium/ Netherlands	100
Flyvefisken	PG/MHC	Denmark	102
Hunt	MCMV	United Kingdom	96
Kingston	MCDV	Canada	94
Laksamana	FSG	Malaysia	97
Lerici/Gaeta	MHC/MSC	Italy	98
Minerva	FS	Italy	92
Niels Juel	FFG	Denmark	90
Osprey	MHC	United States	95
Qahir	FSG	Oman (UK)	89
Sandown	MHC	United Kingdom	103
Rauma	PCFG	Finland	105
Victory	FSG	Singapore	101
Visby	FSG	Sweden	99

Amphibious Warfare Vessels

Name	Type	Country	No.
Albion	LPD	United Kingdom	111
Foudre	LSD	France	114
Ocean	LPH	United Kingdom	110
Osumi	LPD	Japan	115
Ropucha	LST	Russia	117
Rotterdam/Galacia	LPD	Netherlands/Spain	113
San Antonio	LPD	United States	109
San Giorgio	LPD	Italy	116
Tarawa	LHA	United States	108
Wasp	LHD	United States	107
Whidbey Island/ Harpers Ferry	LSD	United States	112

Logistic Support Vessels

Name	Type	Country	No.
Amsterdam/Patiño	AOR	Netherlands/ Spain	123
Argus	ATS	United Kingdom	121
Durance	AOR	France/Australia	122
Endeavour	AOR	New Zealand	125
Etna	AOR	Italy	124
Fort Victoria	AOR	United Kingdom	120
Supply	AOE	United States	119